RickGillis.com

JOB!

Rick Gillis
Edited by Ronni Bennett

With an Introduction by
Chester Elton
New York Times Best-Selling Author
The Carrot Principle, The Orange Revolution,
All In and *What Motivates Me*

For more information, to obtain a media bio or to book the author
visit http://www.RickGillis.com/contact.html
email: info@rickgillis.com

\\\

Job Search | Careers | Employment | Keywords
Resumes | Accomplishments | Social Media in Job Search

ISBN-13: 978-0615514536
ISBN-10: 0615514537
Library of Congress Control Number: 2011912667

Other Books by Rick Gillis

The Real Secret to Finding a Job?
Make Me Money or Save Me Money!

Make Me Money or Save Me Money!
The Real Secret to Finding a Job
for New and Recent College Graduates

Really Useful Job Search Tactics
A Handbook of Contemporary Job Hunting Techniques

Those who say it cannot be done
should get out of the way of those doing it.
–Chinese Proverb

Table of Contents

Chapter 1   The Accomplishments Statement 1

Chapter 2   The Accomplishments Inventory 13

Chapter 3   The Art of Creating an Accomplishment 23

Chapter 4   The Short-Form (or Abbreviated) Resume 35

Chapter 5   Short-Form Resume – The Top Half 45

Chapter 6   Short-Form Resume – The Second Half.................................. 61

Chapter 7   Keywords.. 71

Chapter 8   The Long-Form (or Traditional) Resume 81

Chapter 9   Social Media, LinkedIn and Job Search 89

Chapter 10   Additional Thoughts on This Job Search Thing...................... 95

Chapter 11   The Entry-Level/New College Graduate Resume.................105

Guest Introduction
By Chester Elton

In a time of uncertainty we all look for stability. In our relationships, in where we live, and especially where we work. In fact if we are out of work it impacts everything else in our lives. There is nothing worse than the feeling that you can't, or might not be able to provide for yourself or your family.

What I love about this wonderful book is that it isn't a book so much as a road map. Your own personal road map to get the job you want and a job where you can excel or to take you from where you are now to where you want to be in the near future, in three simple steps. It is common sense put in an easy to follow and implement plan. You will go from "hoping" for a new job to a detailed strategy on how to get that perfect job for you.

Rick Gillis is uniquely qualified to help you make this happen. For years Rick has helped people go from unemployed to working in their dream jobs. He doesn't just give advice from studies and trends he gives you insights from his own life and journey. He has lived what he is teaching in this gem of a book.

Here is a quick tip, think of this book as your treasure map to not just a better job, but also a better life. Take the time to study the principles taught here and don't hesitate to highlight, underline and re-read the sections that will help you the most. This isn't a read once and put it away. It is a carry around with you, read it again kind of book for those of you who are serious about upgrading where you work and how you work.

If you have ever thought you couldn't make the move, or didn't have the confidence to go and get the job you really want, give yourself the best chance by reading this book and making a change in your work and life. Take a chance on yourself by following these proven 3 steps.

Start working towards a better job now. You've already picked up this book. Start reading!

Chester Elton
New York Times Best Selling Co-Author of *The Carrot Principle, The Orange Revolution, All In & What Motivates Me*

Author's Introduction

Following the collapse of the Roman Empire in 476, Western Europe entered a period of cultural decline that came to be known as the Dark Ages.

With the arrival of email, PC's, Mac's, laptops, mobile devices and tablets; the proliferation of job boards and apps as well as video and YouTube interviews (not necessarily in that order), I think it's fair that we can now call the period of job search prior to the personal computer the Dark Ages of Job Search.

How we apply for jobs is continuously mutating but the fundamentals of presenting your value and desire to work for an employer— online or in-person—will never change.

"JOB!" will teach you how to successfully navigate resume filtering software, exploit the online application, get the hiring manager to 'like' you just from reviewing your resume, get you the phone call. The Accomplishments Statement you will learn about in the first three chapters of "JOB!" will motivate you, build confidence and prepare you for the successful interview and salary negotiation to follow.

A Short History of Me

I'm Rick Gillis. I helped launch the first job board in the greater Houston, TX (USA) area in the 1990's. I spent 10 years calling on recruiters, staffing companies, hiring managers and business owners. I called on the smallest of companies and the largest of corporations.

What I learned in that time was that hiring managers want things a certain way and for the most part job seekers don't speak the language of employment. (And why would you? You job is to do your job. Not learn how to find your next job. Or is it...?)

Before long I found myself speaking before job search groups, associations and college audiences who wanted to learn how to use this new 'Internet thing' in their job search which eventually lead to writing my first book, hosting a couple of employment talk radio shows and an employment-based cable TV show. In these various roles (sales guy to TV host) I have interviewed some of the best and brightest on both sides of the issue.

I have created my own resume format: the one-page, Short-Form resume. This format works! Recruiters like it; it successfully navigates resume filtering software and creates the dialog between you and the recruiter necessary for you to get the interview. I know you will be impressed with the simplicity that is the Short-Form resume.

"JOB!" is my way of sharing this information with you. This is a quick read. No nonsense. No fluff. Only the actionable information you need to land your next position.
Your success is my success!

Good Job Hunting!
Rick Gillis
RickGillis.com

Very special thanks to those job seekers I have counseled.
I try to teach you all I can but you have no idea
how much I learn from you.

Job!

Chapter 1

The Accomplishments Statement

"It is hard for an empty bag to stand upright."
Benjamin Franklin

Job search is tough. But it becomes much more straightforward once you know how to successfully navigate the resume filtering and candidate management systems so prolific today. That knowledge in combination with the ability to convince a potential employer of your value will move your candidacy to the top of the list every time. You will find that you are not just being offered another job but receiving real opportunities.

By the time you finish reading this book, you will know how to make this happen.

Keep in mind that you are seeking only one position. You do not, and should not, put too much mental energy into daily news reports about the unemployment rate and the ups and downs of the economy. What you do need to be conscious of is that job search is more highly competitive than it ever has been and job seekers, in my experience, do not know how to compete. I'm going to change that for you.

I will teach you how to compete with "why-hasn't-anyone-told-me-this-before" strategies as well as one fresh new tool and some other innovative techniques that have proved successful with thousands of people who have attended my live presentations, heard me on radio or seen me on TV.

Where NOT to Start

If you are reading this, you are either not working or you are thinking that things are looking tenuous at work. So you whip out your old resume (what I call the "obituary"—but more on that later), or fire up the computer to begin drafting your new resume, right? WRONG!

This is not where you begin your job search, yet it is the place where 99.9 percent of all job seekers start. Instead, here are the 3 steps to your next job. Note that your traditional resume is last.

1. Take a Personal Accomplishments Inventory
2. Write a Short-Form, Resume-Filtering Software Friendly (Accomplishments-Based) Resume
3. Write a Traditional (Long-Form) Resume

I will get to that traditional resume you are familiar with later and it will be easiest one you've ever written. But first:

Resumes are Unfair

I have maintained that resumes are unfair for years. Resumes, as we use them for job search in the United States, are one of the most difficult problems to overcome. Writing a powerful, spot-on resume is a tough assignment.

To understand why resumes are unfair, you must know a little about what most of the rest of the northern hemisphere (Asia, Europe, the Middle East and Africa) use in place of a resume: they use a Curriculum Vitae or CV. This document can be a few pages long or an entire personal biography of hundreds of pages. (About the only place you will see a CV in the U.S. is in academic or scientific circles.) Interestingly, Australia, Mexico, Central and South America prefer the American-style resume.

As a job seeker, your job is to create a dynamic one-page, get-the-recruiter's-attention, Short-Form (or Abbreviated) Resume to be followed up with a longer (two to five pages max) traditional resume that will cause the company to schedule an interview with you. If you're not seeking your first-ever job, you know how hard this is. But if you follow the instructions in this book, the pain of creating your resume will go away. I promise.

Another thing to think about: after all the effort you have made to prepare your resume, you have only three to 10 seconds (that's all!) to make that almighty first impression. In that first glance of your resume, the recruiter must be able to immediately see your value, skills, experience and achievements in such a manner that he or she will consider you a viable candidate to be contacted about the position.

A resume, regardless of length or format, serves only one purpose — to initiate a dialogue. A well-crafted resume will get you the interview. And a good Accomplishments Statement will get you the job.

Now, on to the first of the 3 steps to your next job: Creating your Accomplishments Statement.

What? You never heard of an Accomplishments Statement? Of course you haven't; there has never been one until this book. And it's certainly never been taught in any college or professional job search program you may have participated in. But it is the best new job search tool around and it will place you miles above job seekers who do not have one. Let me explain what it is and how it works.

In these 3 steps, you begin your job search not with a resume, but by taking a personal inventory of what you have to offer an employer by determining the Return On Investment (ROI) that you will provide your next employer. When you speak to the idea that you recognize how expensive it is to run a business on a daily basis, you quickly become compelling and memorable in the mind of a business owner or hiring manager.

One of the sad realities of real-world job search is that too often job seekers stumble through two or more interviews before they begin to "get it" - that is, to understand and implement what it takes to sufficiently impress an interviewer to hire them. This is

Stock Option
To you, your paycheck is payment for services rendered. To an employer, your paycheck is their investment in you. Stated another way—what does an investor do with an underperforming stock? Get the idea?

no longer a problem when you grasp the value of the Accomplishments Statement.

Just One Peril of Not Having an Accomplishments Statement

Imagine you have sailed past hundreds of other applicants. You made it into the interview for that job that has your name all over it. Yeah, baby!

On your way home from the interview you are replaying the details of the give and take in your mind when all of a sudden it hits you (and you begin slamming the steering wheel) that you FORGOT to tell them about the time you _____ (fill in the blank).

And that was the one piece that was going to land you the job. Absolutely, unequivocally would have closed the deal — and you forgot to tell them. You can't call them back and look like an idiot because you forgot to tell them that. You certainly can't drop an email to tell them you forgot. You blew it. You really blew it.

(My advice if you came to me at a time like that would be "what the heck, you already shot yourself in the foot. What have you got to lose? Call 'em.")

But had you prepared an Accomplishments Statement, had you put yourself through this exercise and folded the document into your portfolio to review prior to and even during the interview, this would never have happened.

What the Accomplishments Statement Accomplishes

The Accomplishments Statement does much more than just prepare you to write a compelling, dynamic resume. It prepares you for a successful, preliminary telephone interview and helps you ace the personal, on-site interview. It builds confidence, enhances motivation and overcomes the shock and awe of termination if that is something you have suffered.

Another thing: you want to nail the proverbial 30-second elevator pitch? How about doing it in half the time and knocking the socks off your listener? You will learn to do that by preparing the Accomplishments Statement.

I just told you that I consider resumes to be unfair. The Accomplishments Statement is the great equalizer. It is the document that levels and expands the playing field and does so to your advantage. By creating an Accomplishments Statement you are presenting the "total package of you" to the company for their consideration.

The Accomplishments Statement, besides stating your personal best accomplishments and achievements, also works to minimize age discrimination issues by not dealing in dates, times and places (much more on this later). Instead, it concentrates on what you did at those places, dates and times and the impact you made at each organization.

Not Negotiable

Taking a personal inventory is not negotiable when working with me as a private client. This exercise works! From entry-level job seeker to CEO, I have successfully proven the Accomplishments Statement's effectiveness too many times to count. You could call this aspect of your job search preparation the "heavy lifting" part that will let you sail through steps 2 and 3. But the truth is, it's not difficult at all — it just takes a little time, thought and some minor detective work.

What Will You Do With Your Accomplishments Statement?

When you finish working up your personal inventory, you will prepare this document for presentation. Yup, you will be presenting a copy to everyone you interview with. More on this later but what you need to be aware of now is that you will be formatting your Accomplishments Statement for professional presentation alongside your resume. (You may want to view a sample completed Accomplishments Statement in the Appendix at the back of the book but you will have plenty of time for that as we work together through this process.)

At the Interview

When you have your Accomplishments Statement, go to each and every interview you attend with enough copies for each person with whom you interview. During the interview, when there is a natural place to mention that you have a prepared list of your personal best accomplishments, do so and hand it over.

If there is no comfortable time for you to present it during the interview, there is always a perfect opportunity at the end of the interview when the recruiter (or recruiters) asks if there is anything else you would like them to know about you.

You will say, "Yes, I'd like to leave you with a copy of my personal best accomplishments." First, this is something that in all probability they have never experienced before (it's good to be first!) and second, you have just created a reason to possibly extend the interview. Remember that an interview is nothing more than a conversation between two or more people and the longer this conversation continues the better. (Interviewers are not prone to keep candidates around any longer than necessary.)

Accomplishments that are most appropriate to the position you are seeking will be listed at the top of your Statement followed by those not related directly to your employment history such as involvement in charities and other outside interests. It is not uncommon for a recruiter to work with, for example, a certain charity. This allows the recruiter to learn a little bit more about you and maybe even come to like you more than they already do.

You might be surprised to learn that the achievements on your list will come not only from your work experience but also from academic, athletic, military and volunteer organizations you may have worked with as well as work you may have done with your church, synagogue, mosque or temple.

Have you been involved in any rescue efforts, helped raise money for a school event or a family in need? Do you regularly donate your time to volunteer? All of this counts.

Do you see the value here? And we are just getting started! After having put yourself through the exercise of recall and calling on former employers, friends, family, professors, teachers, clergy and co-workers (details on this in the next chapter), you will have created a pretty good mental picture of what you have been doing all these years, You will be able to visualize the arc that has been your life and, I promise, you WILL be impressed with YOU. Now you have an amazing document that is all about your favorite subject: the history of you.

By the Phone, On the Phone, On Mobile Devices

Once the Accomplishments Statement is complete, place a copy 'by the phone' (for those of you who know what I'm talking about!), on your cellphone, tablet, or any other mobile devices you carry and leave it there. Here is a scenario for you: There is a recruiter out there working your industry and looking for your job skills. Whether you are a welder, a graphic designer or a chief operating officer, there is no difference for the purpose of this illustration. Said recruiter has narrowed her search to 12 resumes (out of hundreds received) that meet the minimum requirements for the opening she needs to fill. (Later in the book you will learn how to become one of those chosen 12.)

The hiring manager has specifically asked the recruiter to try to find someone with "something extra on the ball, someone who seems to really know what they are doing."

She has already called eight candidates, introduced herself by title and company and has asked each candidate to tell her a little about themselves. And to each query she has received the same nondescript response: "What would you like to know about me?"

In her mind, she is thinking OMG! Don't these people remember where they have applied? Don't they keep a list of some sort so that when/if somebody calls…?

No. Most job seekers are not that efficient.

But YOU, after finishing your Accomplishments Statement and placing it by the phone and/or on your mobile devices receive a call from the same recruiter and upon being asked to tell her about yourself, look to your Accomplishments Statement and reading from the top of the list, say, "Well, I'd like you to know about the time that I was responsible for_____which resulted in _____. Is that something you would like to know more about?" (You will soon learn how to fill in the blanks.)

Wow! You, dear job seeker, have just hit a recruiting grand slam. You have instantly become compelling and memorable. You will get an opportunity to interview in person.

In my experience, there are not many people prepared to deal with an employment opportunity the moment it makes itself apparent. (For the purpose of this illustration, I use the phone call. It could just as easily be at a job fair, a networking environment or even a business lunch that such a moment happens).

The Accomplishments Statement prepares you for this moment. You won't be the person struggling to think of something bright to say because you have prepared for this eventuality. You are prepared to say exactly the right thing.

Now, let's get to the nuts and bolts of creating your Accomplishments Statement.

Harrumph!

"I remember all the important stuff in
my career—why would I go to all this trouble?"

Know that some of my greatest successes in job search counseling
have been helping people land in the C-suite with salaries they would
be comfortable talking about on Wall Street. Whoever you are reading
this book, entry-level job seeker or seasoned professional,
I stake my professional reputation on the value of this process.

Job!

Chapter 2

The Accomplishments Inventory

"You can have everything in life you want if you will just help other people get what they want."
Zig Ziglar

"How did I make a difference?"

Your ability to answer that question, first for yourself and then for potential employers, is the key to your professional success.

In today's competitive workplace, it is not enough to know how to do the job. You must be able to convince a recruiter or hiring manager that you will bring value to your next employer's company. Until someone can verify that you can walk the walk (known as the probationary period), you had better be able to talk the talk to get a chance to prove yourself. Let me show you what I mean.

The Hardware Store

Several years ago while I was speaking before a large group of people about job search, I could tell they were not grasping the idea of thinking of themselves as a value proposition. It was then that I recalled the first time I used my personal value statement to land the job.

This idea of value came easily to me because I had worked in the family hardware store from the time I was a kid. I learned early that if we didn't sell something that day, my dad and I might not stop at the market on the way home that evening.

By the time I graduated from high school, we had closed the store and I went out looking for my first "real job." A new lumber yard was going up nearby and, deciding that's where I wanted to work; I put on my best suit (probably my only suit) and made my way to the employment office.

What a goof! I stood out like a sore thumb! Every guy in line looked like Marlon Brando in the *On The Waterfront* movie: jeans and white T-shirts with a pack of cigarettes rolled up in one sleeve. These were working guys. They were darkened by the sun and their hands were calloused. Many of them wore scuffed hardhats and had a pair of well-worn, work gloves shoved into their back pockets.

So here I come, 18 years old, in my best suit thinking I'm "all that" and that this was how you applied for a job. (It is, by the way.) I filled out the application and stood in another line for my interview. When my turn came, I could tell from the look on the yard manager's face that I was a bit overdressed for the job. It was evident he thought I wasn't "tough enough" for the position. But it was what I said that cocked his eyebrow. I told him that for every dollar he paid me I would give him back ten.

Slowly and without saying a word he reached behind him, grabbed a pair of work gloves along with a hardhat and, tossing them across the desk, told me to report in at 7AM the next morning. I still remember the look of skepticism on Mr. Cordell Dykes' face. I worked for him for better than a year before moving on.

I told this story to the group and I saw they "got it." Why tell you this? Because based on that one line, $10 for each $1 paid, Mr. Dykes took a chance on me. Of course, I also had to deliver, which I did.

You already know your own story (or stories) that will land you your next opportunity. You just need to uncover them.

Getting Started with Your Accomplishments Statement

Your Accomplishments Statement is a formal job search document, as important as

Job Search is Sales. So is Dating.

From time to time, I hear from job seekers that they don't sell. Well, gang, it's time to blow that concept out of the water. You want a job? You sell. It's that simple. You are the product and you are the best model available this season!

Think back to a time when you were trying to woo that someone special. (In its purest form, dating is sales. You are selling you. That first nervous phone call? Consider it the equivalent of the cold call.)

When I was in the online job board business, I compared our employment site to dating sites. "We hope you meet and greet," I used to say, "kiss on the first date and go on to make babies... but we're just here to make the introduction."

The interview is the corporate version of the first date. Everyone is on their best behavior.

See where I'm going here? Were you to apply all the energy and creativity that you applied in your efforts to attract that someone special to your job search...just imagine.

your resume. While your resume's sole purpose is to initiate an introduction between you and someone interested in hiring you, the Accomplishments Statement, offered at the right moment, serves an equally important purpose. The Accomplishments Statement more fully depicts you as a complete package in a manner that a resume is not designed to do.

Your goal in crafting a dynamic Accomplishments Statement, regardless of your age and experience, is to identify, at minimum, four exceptional professional achievements – each one relevant to what you do in your field of expertise.

If you are the CEO of a multinational corporation, then you should be able to pull your accomplishments from all those articles they wrote about you in *Bloomberg Business Week* or *The Wall Street Journal*.

As an admin assistant or a skilled trades professional, your accomplishments will focus on how you added value as a result of your ability to work smarter, faster and more efficiently. I'm pleased when counseling someone to learn that, upon their departure, the company was forced to replace them with more than one person. I actually know of one organization that was required to replace a director with 12 people! That was expensive!

Accomplishments Part One: From Memory
Accomplishments come from two places. The first is from you—right out of your memory.

Begin compiling your accomplishments by taking out paper and pen or opening up a computer document and just begin typing away. The best place to start is your work history; get out that resume you need to update for this job search.

Go through each job entry and recall all the things you are proud of, things that made a difference, that added value to the company. Did you increase sales? Find a way to shorten the time to market? Improve an inventory system? Were you involved in crafting a successful marketing plan or develop a piece of software that was actually implemented into the corporate process? Keep writing. It doesn't matter how many accomplishments you have - the more, the better. (Entry-level job seeker accomplishments are discussed in more detail in the last chapter of the book.)

For now, write down the entire story associated with each accomplishment – what you did, how you did it and how the company benefited from your effort. This is rich training for interviewing and it's a great motivational exercise to build personal confidence. You will be amazed as you find yourself remembering other achievements while jotting down the particulars of another. When you are done, you won't believe how good you will feel about you. Cool, huh?

But wait. A lot of job seekers balk at this step. They showed up and did what they were supposed to do which, they say, was nothing spectacular. Oh, yeah? Let me give you an example of someone I counseled who did not realize how much value he brought to his former position as a result of doing little more than what he was supposed to do!

The Payroll Clerk

I'll call my client David since that is his real name. David came to me and said he had been going crazy trying to come up with even one accomplishment he was proud enough of to list on his Accomplishments Statement. He and I sat down and after about 45 minutes of what felt like pulling teeth, I finally asked him (fairly shouting) "David! There MUST be at least one thing you have done on the job that you were proud of!"

David is a payroll clerk and as such he just didn't feel he had brought that much value to his company (which in this case was a global energy company). David's problem was that he was only one among the many payroll clerks in the office, just another cog in the machine. Or so he thought.

After a while, David sheepishly mentioned that he was, "kind of proud of the fact that I had zero returns on my first payroll of 6,000."

I nearly fell off my seat! 6000 paychecks! THIS is what I had been looking for. Think about it: you don't mess with people's money. Ever. You don't mess with their vacation time, withholding, benefits or taxes. David had struck gold. But in his mind (and in reality), he had "just" been doing what he was supposed to do.

But which payroll clerk would you hire? The guy who could handle the details associated with preparing a payroll of 6000 checks and making no mistakes the first time out or the guy who can't tell you what he can do for your company? The choice is obvious. I want the guy who will save me money by getting it right.

Accomplishments Part Two: Colleagues' Memories

The next step is one of the most important in this process. It will take more time and more effort than part one, but because the accomplishments come from other people, it is even more rewarding.

Reach out to family, fellow students, former co-workers, supervisors, bosses and colleagues. Even customers, clients and vendors are a good source. Ask each of them if they can recall a time when they were involved in a work activity with you when you did something that made an impact on them. The responses will work to jog your memory about other things you've forgotten. Other times, the answers will surprise you as people recount how you impressed them.

As the stories come in, write them down on your growing list including, as in part one, what you did, how you did it and what the result was for the company. For now don't worry about how the Statement looks or reads. You are collecting the inventory you will be working with. Just get down the details. The how, what, where, when, and why. We'll lay it all out professionally in the next chapter.

Accomplishments Part Three: Personal Accomplishments

In my opinion we too often lose sight of job seeking from the recruiter's point of view. Keep in mind that when you first meet and greet a recruiter, it is not their job to like you. Not because they aren't good people but because they can't; they have to say "no" to so many applicants.

These same recruiters also have real lives outside the office. Going a step further than the competition by presenting personal accomplishments from interests beyond the scope of your work, you will find yourself connecting with recruiters on a level that any person not using the Accomplishments Statement can't easily do. This connection is not to be taken lightly. It can make the difference between getting a chance for a second interview and not.

This is not to take away from the fact that you first have to be able to prove that you are qualified for the job. But with the level of competition and the number of talented people interviewing for the same jobs, this part asks what you can do to set yourself apart after you have established your professional bona fides.

In this exercise, add the personal accomplishments you remember and/or feel good about related to your involvement with charities or times you volunteered. Then add accomplishments related to current and past academic, athletic, military or religious organizations you have been involved with.

Then, as with your professional accomplishments, reach out to people you volunteered with, to professors, teachers, religious leaders, coaches and, most importantly, family and friends. Ask each of them if they can recall a time when they were involved in an activity with you in which you made an impact on them. If you have children (regardless of their age), listen closely to them. I promise the stuff they tell you will floor you. Add all these to your growing accomplishments list.

I regularly hear back from candidates I have worked with who tell me things like, "Her son and mine went to the same school" or "Turns out he was very interested in sailing and wanted to know more about my racing team" or "It just so happens that he was involved in a major fund raiser for the American Cancer Society too." Each of those instances opens the door a little wider to your next job.

Lastly, don't forget to ask you mom! I'm not joking here. Your mom will remember stuff that you have told her along the way about school, volunteer activities and on the job. For the entry-level job seeker moms are an invaluable source of accomplishments.

How Many Personal Accomplishments?

There is no limit to the number of personal accomplishments you will compile while taking your inventory. You are limited only by life experience. If you are a mature job seeker you have no excuse not to create a minimum of 20. If you are a recent graduate, your list will be shorter but at your age, you can include high school achievements or activities that indicate such factors as leadership. Young people, in my experience, always have more to offer than they think they do and when I work with them, we can generally find eight to 10 genuine, solid accomplishments for their list. (The last chapter of the book is dedicated to Entry-level job seeker issues, content and formatting.)

He Saved the Company—And Would Never Have Known If He Hadn't Asked!

Although it may seem daunting (it's not) to contact former employers, colleagues, coaches and volunteer leaders along with family and friends, customers and clients, the payoff can be astonishing, as it was with Joe.

At one of my full-day workshops, he came up to me to apologize for texting while I was speaking. Joe said that he had been so taken with the idea of learning what impact he might have made on companies where he had been employed that he had sent a text to ten co-workers including his previous boss. Within minutes he received a text back from his former employer stating that he had saved the company. What?!

At the break, Joe called his former boss and asked him what he meant in his text. It turned out that the company had been in dire straits and on the brink of failure. His boss couldn't tell anyone for fear they would leave which would mean immediate failure. He went on to tell Joe that the product and plan Joe developed at that moment in time, as well as his implementation, oversight, and follow through, had saved the company! The company is still in business and, just FYI, the reason Joe was attending one of my workshops was because he formally retired from this company. After deciding that retirement was not his thing, he determined to hone his job search skills and explore new opportunities.

Had Joe not asked his former employer what difference he had made while on the job, he would have never known about the incident that came to be the first one listed on his Accomplishments Statement.

Joe presented his Accomplishments Statement at his next interview. As a result he is now a program manager in the corporate division of one of the largest community colleges in the nation.

Job!

Chapter 3

The Art of Creating an Accomplishment

"I always turn to the sports pages first, which records
people's accomplishments.
The front page has nothing but man's failures."
Earl Warren

The Parking Lot Cashier

A middle-aged woman called to ask what she could possibly do to improve her circumstances. She had been a parking lot cashier for a major hospital in the Texas Medical Center for 17 years. After asking her to tell me what she was most proud of over such a long period of time, she said she had had an out-of-balance cash drawer only twice in all those years and had earned attendance awards for having never missed a day of work.

Again, I bring to your attention that doing what you are supposed to do and doing it well is a justifiable accomplishment.

I worked with this lady and together we crafted a resume that focused on her accomplishments which were based on reliability, responsibility, honesty and trustworthiness! We noted her attendance and cash drawer accomplishments.

Not altogether surprising, she did not go out and get a new job with another employer. Instead, she used her newly created accomplishments-based resume to go back to her current employer to find her next job. She was advanced into a better paying, more responsible position within the hospital.

That story should help make it obvious that the effort you put into your Accomplishments Statement plays a major role in how your resume will read, whatever your level of experience. What you are learning here will guide you into crafting an accomplishments-based resume that will make a positive impact on the person reviewing it.

By now, you should have your list of 10 to 20+ accomplishment stories. With that, get a clean sheet of paper or open a new page on your computer. We are going to refine these stories into powerful bullet points that will make a recruiter or hiring manager sit up and pay attention – and get you that all-important telephone call.

How do you do this? By understanding the three components of a great accomplishment.

An Equal and Opposite Reaction

Every good book, movie, TV show or song has a beginning, a middle and an end that brings the story or idea to a satisfying conclusion. So too does a well-written accomplishment. The only difference is that we will call the conclusion of an accomplishment a net result—the part that indicates how you made a difference and why an employer should take a chance by placing you on the payroll.

Sales people are accustomed to providing a NET RESULT for every entry on a resume. Regardless of what you do for a living, you must to learn to do the same. Every accomplishment must show how you made the company money or saved the company money.

For example, I'm looking at a paralegal's resume and I see that he "created a filing system." Nothing more, nothing less, just: "I created a filing system." To that I say — as will all recruiters — so what?! You must not have done such a great job on the "ol' filing system" since here you are looking for a new job.

But what if that paralegal told me instead that he had "Created a filing system resulting in 300 man hours saved per week." Now *that's* an eye-opener.

Let's break that statement down by beginning, middle and end or net result:

Beginning:	Created a filing system
Middle:	resulting in
End/Net Result:	300 man hours saved per week.

Now, as the hiring manager, I have something I can sink my teeth into. And more importantly, I want to learn more about how you did this. To do so requires that I take action — most likely by placing a phone call.

Remember
You are not looking for a job.
You are looking for
a phone call.

If you take nothing else away from this book, please take
"resulting in" with you.
These two words are the middle of any accomplishment;
set up the net result and are golden!
Use them, complete the sentence and you have created
a proper accomplishment.
(You may also begin an accomplishment with
"As a result of…" for variety.)
This suggestion will serve you well in performance
reviews as well as job search.

Age Discrimination & Accomplishments
Before we go any further, let's talk briefly about age discrimination. As I have said in previous books, age discrimination is exceptionally difficult to prove on the job and virtually impossible to prove in job search. For now, that is unlikely to change; it is what it is, so let's deal with it. Minimizing age discrimination for mature job seekers is one of my foremost goals in coaching job seekers. I doubt anyone else has ever taken the position of developing tools specifically for the mature job seeker.

Where Did I...? When Did I...?

"Responsible for 49% of all sales resulting in approximately $1,000,000 net to the company."

This is one of my personal accomplishments. Re-read it and then answer this question: Where and when did I do what I said I did?

You don't know because I did not tell you.

By deliberately removing date, time and/or place, no one has any idea if I achieved this accomplishment when I was 25 or 35 or 45 or 55 or... As a result, if the recruiter is interested in pursuing me based on this entry in my resume, she will need to call me to learn more. And what have I previously told you about the function of my accomplishments-based resume? It serves no other purpose than to create a dialogue.

So how does this effort minimize age discrimination? After all, you will still be placing dates of employment on your resume that will obviously allow the reader to, at minimum, guesstimate your age. Well, based on my resume model, they may have to keep guessing—but we'll get to that in Chapter 6 where I'll explain in detail the actual placement of accomplishments and the age minimization process in your resume at that time.

For now, as you remove date/time/place from your accomplishments list, you must ask yourself (and be truthful): Can I still accomplish what I state in my Accomplishments Statement and, later, my resume? If not, do not use it! Once you make any kind of assertion on your resume, it is rightfully regarded by hiring managers as gospel. The relevance lies in the fact that you can still do it. If you can't walk-the-walk, don't talk about it - at least, not on your Accomplishments Statement and resume.

Qualifying/Quantifying Your Net Result

Often, people tell me they can't quantify how they "saved the company money or made the company money." To this I say, bull!

You may be able to determine the value you added to your previous organization by just asking! It's certainly no stretch these days to say that many of you lost previous jobs through no fault of your own due to the economy. If this is the case, contact your former supervisor and ask what you contributed to the bottom line while on staff. You could be pleasantly surprised with the response.

On the other hand, if you don't have a friendly tie to the company or for whatever reasons you can't obtain an answer to the value you delivered in hard numbers, use powerful (but accurate!), descriptive language to show your value. An example: "I created a filing system that resulted in a more managed and efficient delivery of client files to attorneys and support staff."

Fine Tune Your Accomplishments for Presentation

You might decide to list the name of the companies or organizations with your accomplishments—especially if they have real name-dropper value. It's your choice, but my preference is to save it for the phone interview.

The Final Step: Creating Your Accomplishments Statement

Now it's your turn. Go through each accomplishment description on your list one by one. Remove date/time/place and break them down into new, short, provocative, net-result, accomplishment statements. Note that the middle is always the same, "resulting in."

Dollar Signs, Percentage Symbols & Zeros

As much as possible use **$** and **%** symbols when drafting your accomplishments—they jump off the page.

When it comes to describing dollar amounts, always **"Spell Out The Zeros!"**

$3.2 Million or $3.2MM is not nearly as attention grabbing as **$3,200,000!**

This applies to all your job search documentation—the Accomplishments Worksheet, the Short-Form Resume, the Long-Form Resume and any other documents or applications you may be asked to provide.

Condense each of your accomplishments into a single, bullet-point statement. Your goal here is to reduce your original accomplishment description to its essence. You will use these in your Short-Form resume. Keep them as short as possible providing only that information necessary to earn a hiring manager's interest.

Look back at my "49% of sales" accomplishment and recognize how this statement is only the beginning of an entire discussion I could have during an interview on how we grew the company.

You have already seen this before but I think it worth repeating: "Responsible for _____ which resulted in _____." Fill in the blanks keeping your accomplishment to a single sentence if possible.

When you have finished writing all your accomplishment statements, choose those achievements that will rate highest with a recruiter seeking to fill the position you desire. Organize your accomplishments not chronologically but in order of significance to the interview and the position you are seeking.

Your completed document may have an accomplishment from 2014 in the first position, one from 2001 in the second position followed by one achieved in 2006. Remember, this is not about when you achieved but rather that you are capable of doing the deal now—regardless of your age. (Later, you might revise the order again to tailor the document for another position you are applying for.)

Now, after giving your document a title (something like "Rick Gillis Personal Accomplishments") and adding your contact information (phone and email only), list your rewritten and rearranged accomplishments. Do not number them. All of your accomplishments are equally important. By numbering them a recruiter will think the first item listed is the most important and not necessarily review the rest of your Statement. Use bullets and skip a line between each accomplishment. Allow for white space. Make it easy to read. (See the Accomplishments Statement sample in the Appendix.)

Summing Up
When we begin drafting your Short-Form Resume, you will quickly see how all your hard work here pays off. You have completed the heavy lifting part of the entire process. Your biggest concern going forward will be formatting since most of the information you require can be

found in your current obituary—er, I mean, your existing resume and on your newly created Accomplishments Statement.

The grand exclamation point to this first step of the 3 steps to your next job will happen when a hiring manager, reviewing your resume (and your Accomplishments Statement) asks, "How did you do that?" Remember: the real question behind the question is, "Can you do that for me?!"

This Exercise is Really Much Bigger Than You Think

All this work is not being undertaken solely for your current job search. It really is much bigger than that. The Accomplishments Statement is a "living document." What I hope to instill in you is a desire to continue this effort for a lifetime. Think of employment as athletic competition. The business owner is the coach and has no choice but to field the very best team possible. On the day the boss determines you are no longer capable of carrying your own weight (when you are no longer making or saving the company money), your time is up. (Remember the "Stock Option" sidebar in Chapter 1? What do you do with an under-performing stock in your portfolio?) This is the moment when your journal may play a pivotal role as evidence of your specific value to the organization today, yesterday and last year. Make up your mind now to compile and keep an accomplishments journal.

• • •

The Skeptical MBA (for my Young Readers)

I could tell Jason, a newly-minted MBA, was skeptical. He honestly thought that those three letters following his name on his resume would be his ticket to a thriving career. On top of this, Jason genuinely thought that prior to completing his master's degree he had no accomplishments worthy of discussion.

After several months with few interviews and no job, Jason came to me for help and I agreed on the condition that he wholeheartedly embrace my Accomplishments Statement process.

Jason had minimal employment history but he had extensive experience playing and coaching little league soccer.

As part of taking his personal assessment, he called former coaches, instructors and professors. The list he compiled was rich—and previously unknown to Jason! What he learned was that he was recognized by virtually everyone he contacted as a natural leader, a responsible, take-charge kind of guy willing to go the extra mile when necessary. I couldn't have agreed more.

We produced a respectable Accomplishments Statement not heavily based in career history—simply because Jason had no career history to speak of. (This is exactly the problem that all young job seekers have; they need the experience to get the job but they need the job to get the experience.)

We next created his resume and I launched Jason back into the street. Within three months, Jason was hired over several other candidate finalists as a business analyst at one of the largest business printing companies in the world. He received other offers along the way but he held out for the one he wanted—and he got it!

Jason told me he had been able to express his leadership skills, his motivation and personal desire to bring value to the company based on all he had learned compiling his personal accomplishments. In interviews, he was able to state specific instances when he had taken charge on the soccer field both as a player and coach, and how those experiences had prepared him for a successful college career and now the business world.

See the Appendix for Janet Job Seeker's completed

Accomplishments Worksheet

or visit www.RickGillis.com

for samples of all

documents mentioned in

Job!

Job!

Chapter 4

The Short-Form (or Abbreviated) Resume

"Insanity: Doing the same thing over and over again and expecting different results."
Albert Einstein

Congratulations, you have completed your Accomplishments Statement! Most importantly, you have assembled the information that will be the foundation of your Short-Form Resume and the heavy lifting is done. Creating your resume is now little more than a matter of thoughtful execution.

The Short-Form Resume Overview

Because the idea of a Short-Form Resume is probably new to you, let me tell you its importance to your success in finding a job. I designed the Short-Form Resume to fulfill these criteria:

- To impress professional recruiters with the focused, razor-sharp information it contains
- To minimize age-discrimination (for young and mature job seekers alike)
- To successfully navigate the resume filtering software that can keep your resume out of the hands of recruiters

The Short-Form Resume, in a significant departure from traditional resumes, is also designed to address your future with the company because although job seekers usually look to the past in their resumes, employers look to the future – and so will your new resume.

•   •   •

Note: During the reading of this and the following chapters you may wish to review the sample Short-Form/Abbreviated Resume that follows or you can refer to the Appendix at the back of the book for an additional copy of the same document.

•   •   •

Jerry Job Seeker

JerryJobSeeker@email.com　　　　　　　　　　　　　　　　　212.456.7890
Willing to Relocate/Travel 70%　　　　　　　　　Currently residing in Houston, TX
Bilingual (English/Spanish)　　　　　　　　　　　　　　　　　Non-smoker

**I am seeking the position of International Sales Manager for
Giant Industrial Corporation reference #12345**

Objective Statement

As a result of my skills, experience and education I am capable of significantly increasing net revenue by implementation of innovative, proven management, motivational and sales training techniques.

Selected Accomplishments

- Inherited and then overcame a $5,000,000 deficit in a badly designed national sales promotion by completely redesigning and developing a far superior plan resulting in a new system that reduced typical man hours the sales staff devoted to plan by 23% while increasing sales in excess of $1,000,000 per quarter.
- Saved over $500,000 annually in key sales communication systems and national transportation expenses while improving level of service to clientele.
- Dramatically reduced sales staff turnover by 28% due to more focused recruiting and selection process. Enhanced training and the creation of targeted management groups resulting in countless man-hour savings.
- Analyzed and merged more than 14 compensation plans into one corporate plan that resulted in a savings exceeding $270,000 the following fiscal year while continuing to fairly compensate the sales staff for their efforts.

Employment History

Giant National Employment Website, Atlanta, GA　　　　　　　Jan 2002 – Present
　　　　Director, West Coast Sales
Giant National Employment Website is recognized as the world's leading employment website.
Gulf Coast Group Internet, Houston, TX　　　　　　　　　　　1998 - 2001
　　　　Sales Manager, South Central US
Texas based Gulf Coast Group is one of the nation's leading providers of employment technology solutions offering full-service employment management systems as well as social media expertise.
The Express Internet Company, New Orleans, LA　　　　　　　1997 – 1998
　　　　Employment Internet Startup Consultant
The Express Internet Company, operating primarily in the Southeastern US, offers turnkey Internet services from web design to network applications.

Bachelor of Science Management, Park University, Parkville, MO
Veteran USAF, Honorable Discharge
Member, Board of Directors, Ronald McDonald House

Keywords: Sales marketing advertising networking consumer retention consumer survey website development website sales internet sales return on investment promotional campaign Houston, TX administrative assistant 3 years' experience articulate attention to detail multi-task professional appearance strong business etiquette college degree word excel power point quicken macromedia contribute bilingual

• • •

No Company Hires Because They "Want To"
No business, large or small, hires frivolously. They can't afford to!

Whether the need is in the mail room, on the sales team or in the C-Suite, there is always, at the core of the decision to hire, a problem that needs to be solved.

You already know it is your job to go into an interview prepared to state your value to the company. Another way of achieving this task is to ask what problem the company is trying to solve.

Is it purely a vacancy or is there an issue at hand that you as an experienced professional can successfully address?

Solve the problem—get the job.

Too Heavy — Too Thin

Another benefit of the Short-Form, one-page resume is that the format will help you avoid what I call the "too heavy—too thin" syndrome.

Often I see resumes that offer up so much information, a recruiter is overwhelmed and can say "no" to the candidate without so much as a phone call. I mean, does an employer really need to know that you graduated summa cum laude—in the 8th grade?! (I'm not making that up. He was 50-some years old.)

On the other hand, I regularly see resumes that are so "thin" (lacking information) that I call them Lists. Lists are pointless.

The Media Tease

Your Short-Form Resume serves a function similar to the technique employed by television and radio hosts as they approach a commercial break. We've all heard, "Don't touch that remote! When we come back we'll teach you how to become a millionaire!" or "Lose 30 pounds in 30 days! How one woman did it — right after this commercial break!"

This hook is called the "tease" and it works. Your Short-Form Resume is your job search "tease" and your target is the hiring manager whose attention you want.

The process goes something like this: the hiring manager receives your Short-Form Resume and calls you to say he likes what he sees but he "needs more information." Yeah baby! The tease worked! You have accomplished your goal — you have initiated a dialog.

Having anticipated this call, your response will be, "Knowing how busy you are, I submitted my Short-Form Resume (or you may choose to use the phrase 'Abbreviated Resume') for your initial consideration." In your very next breath you will ask the recruiter for his email address so you can send over your Long-Form Resume or your regular resume "while we are on the phone."

This is the all-important goal of the Short-Form Resume – to catch that hiring manager's or recruiter's attention so that you break through the crush of other resumes and reach the first step toward your next job – a live telephone conversation.

When to Submit the Short-Form vs. the Long-Form Resume

I am frequently asked when to submit the Short-Form Resume. The answer is to use my "By Invitation or By Introduction" rule. The function of the Short-Form Resume, as you know, is to get someone's attention after which you follow up with your Long-Form Resume providing the recipient with more detailed information. The "By Invitation" aspect of my rule states that if someone asks you to submit your resume for consideration—say a recruiter or someone you met at a conference—submit your Long-Form Resume. "By Introduction" means that if someone offers to hand-carry or electronically forward your resume to a potential employer on your behalf, submit your Long-Form. Whenever you know for certain that a *real, human-person* is on the other end of that email address always, always, always go in with your best job search tool, the Long-Form Resume. In all other instances, *initiate* your job search process with the Short-Form Resume. And the follow up question? What about job boards and online application systems? Go with the Short-Form. When you post your resume to a job board or apply through a company's online process, you are better off when they like what they see but "need more information" necessitating that golden phone call.

Short-Form Resume: One Page Only – Here's Why

When I began calling on hiring professionals, I was immediately struck by the disconnect between what job seekers think will get a recruiter's attention and what recruiter's actually require. Generally, this comes from the candidates' lack of knowledge about what hiring managers need to see to get their attention at the outset. That being the case, one of my goals is to make you "friendly" to recruiters - on paper or online. I want them to like you. We accomplish this by submitting a resume without a lot of frivolous information.

Recruiters are overwhelmed with hundreds and even thousands of resumes, solicited and unsolicited. As a result, people who review resumes for a living have developed the ability to decide yes or no in a matter of seconds. It is therefore mandatory that you make a positive impact in the first 3 to 10 seconds. (Disregard the old saying that you have 30 seconds to make an impression with your resume. That is so 1985! In reality, you get either a 10-second glance or 10 minutes of analytical review.)

Who Ever Said You Must Submit a New Resume for Each Position You Apply For?

Looking for work is tough! Crafting a separate document for each job you apply for is time consuming and the return can be less than zero. The Short-Form format allows you to apply to several positions with minimum modifications to the body of the document. This saves you time and makes your search more efficient.

Career Change/Focusing on Transferable Skills

Since accomplishments reside at the core of the Short-Form Resume, it's the ideal format to submit if you are seeking a career change. The layout allows you to organize those accomplishments to highlight skills that would be of most interest to an employer in a different field. In other words, the Short-Form Resume is the ideal tool to focus on your transferable skills.

Online Applications

There are too many kinds of online job applications to review them all. However, the takeaway is that you should treat an online application with the same "save the company money or make the company money," you-are-the-solution-to-the-problem mindset you bring to your resume and Accomplishments Statement. All the information you have learned up to this point (especially the Accomplishments Statement) and all that follows will serve you well when you are confronted with no other option but to apply for a position through the company's online application system.

General Formatting Rules

Unfortunately for the creative types reading this book (especially you graphic artists), the Short-Form Resume must be produced, as you can see in the sample above, in a "boring," conservative style. This is not because I'm trying to keep you from expressing your design chops but rather because most, if not all, of the filtering software will reject your resume out of hand if it does not meet traditional, business-dictated document formatting. You will have plenty of opportunity to present your Long-Form graphic-wonder in person or when invited to submit your follow-up, Long-Form Resume.

Warning!

It is important that you recognize that most resume filtering software and all job board/resume posting services *re-format your resume* into the font, color and type size chosen by the company.

This means that if you intend to sneak any terms in via the old *white-out technique,* your resume will, in all likelihood, be categorically *rejected from consideration.*

Here are some important points necessary to creating a filtering software-friendly resume:

- Choose a conservative font such as Verdana, Arial, Tahoma or Calibri. I have been advised that Serif fonts (i.e. Times Roman or Cambria) may be rejected by screening software. I have no proof of that—especially since Times Roman has always been a 'go to' font for legal documents—but feel comfortable saying that as long as you choose a font that is clean and easy to read, you should have no problem.
- Similarly do not use any script fonts.
- The smallest font size to use for the body of your resume should be 11 point but if you need to squeeze in a wee bit more information, you might go with a 10.5 point. Any smaller and you're probably asking for trouble by providing more information than is the "standard" for my Short-Form Resume.
- No graphics or logos.
- Do not format using tables.
- No borders.
- For a highly professional appearance, consider using the full margin justification option available in your word processing tool bar. The justification of both left and right margins makes for an authoritative presentation.
- Do not use a header or footer for important information. Filtering software can be set to ignore headers and footers so there is the risk of submitting a "headless" document if you place your contact information in the header (a very common practice) after the software performs its scanning magic.
- A one-inch margin top and bottom is best, larger if you have less information to place on your resume.

- Do not use any lines that cross the entire page from margin to margin. Underscore (underlining), <u>such as this</u> is fine but some filters have been created that will reject a document for nothing more than having a single line run continuously across the page like this:

That about covers the Don'ts. Being the creative person you are, you may think these rules create too dry a document but it's for all the right reasons - like getting you the interview.

The Most Important Part of Your Resume

What is the most important part of your Short-Form Resume? Definitely, the top half. In fact, some would even say the top one third. Think about where your thumb lands when you pick up a piece of paper. Usually right in the middle of the page. Think about the top half of a newspaper — the important, major stories are above the fold and it is the same at websites — it's what's above the scroll that counts.

The next chapter is devoted to the all-important top half of your Short-Form Resume. That will be followed by; you guessed it, the bottom half of the Short-Form Resume which has its own important function to serve.

Job!

Chapter 5

Short-Form Resume – The Top Half

"Take calculated risks. That is quite different from being rash."
George S. Patton

The top half of any resume is the most important part. It is the section that will extend that 10-second review to 10 minutes of examination followed by a phone call. The top half of your Short-Form Resume consists of the following:

•	The Header	Your contact information and much more
•	Your Seeking Statement	A new section you have never before *seen but vital*
•	Your Objective Statement	The opportunity to address your future value
•	Your Selected Accomplishments	You created the list—now let's put it to good use

As we work through each of these crucial sections, it will help you to refer to the sample Short-Form Resume in the previous chapter or the sample in the back of the book. You can also visit www.RickGillis.com at any time and click on the Resume Format tab in the navigation bar for access to all documents mentioned in this book.

The Short-Form Resume Header

Jerry Job Seeker

JerryJobSeeker@email.com
Willing to Relocate/Travel 70%
Bilingual (English/Spanish)

212.456.7890
Currently residing in Houston, TX
Non-smoker

What do you think is the most useless piece of information on a resume? I would not be surprised if it upsets you to learn that it is your name. Here's why.

An employer is concerned daily with issues such as the economy, her workforce, payroll, receivables, payables, taxes, inventory, equipment, software, the competition - the list is endless. On top of that, here come 200 resumes submitted for that analyst position HR posted yesterday. Do you really think your name means anything at this point? No. Not yet.

Remember that until a person reviews your resume and recognizes that you may be the person capable of handling the position they need to fill, he or she will only be taking a quick glance at your name.

A rookie mistake made by entry-level job seekers is posting their name in a 36-point (or larger), bold font. This tactic may actually hurt the applicant since some filtering software rejects resumes based on overly large fonts alone. So post your name top and center in a smart, crisp 14-point font. Smaller is okay too.

Home Address as Disqualifier

You might notice that I do not offer a home address on my resume format and I recommend you don't either. Which leads me to ask why do people place their home address on a resume? "Because that's the way it's always been?" But your physical address may be an automatic disqualifier and this is a secret recruiters prefer that you not know. Let me explain.

I have personally watched as qualified resumes were red-lined for no other reason than that the candidate lived "too far away from the job." Further, the rationale goes, "If I hire that person, he will spend the next 90 days on my payroll seeking a job closer to home." You have to admit there is some sense to this reasoning but it categorically disqualifies the person who may have been willing to relocate to be closer to the job or can carpool, etc.

Allow me to step up on my soapbox for a moment and shout at the world about placing your home address on a resume. Let's say that I walked up to you at the mall and asked you for your home address. Would you give it to me? Of course not! Suffice to say that I don't agree with placing your home address on a resume for either of these reasons.

So what do you put in this space instead? Here are several possibilities:

- If you are willing to work only in and around the area where you live, place the name of your town or city but not your street address.
- If you do not want to miss out on any opportunities regardless of where they might be located in the greater metropolitan area, list the name of the most prominent city in your area in the place of your street address. For example, I live outside Houston. I would place "Houston" on my resume. When the call came from an interested party asking what part of town I live in (and that would be one of the first questions asked as a result of my being deliberately unclear), I would respond with a question of my own: Where is the job located? When the answer came back that the job was clear across town I would say "No problem. I can make it." I would not be willing to pass up any opportunity–nor should you. It could be worth relocating.
- If you are willing to work anywhere in the nation or would consider an expatriate opportunity, omit any reference to your current location altogether.

Your Address and the Online Application

When it comes to applying via an online application process, you have no choice but to answer such questions as your home address. This applies to your address, previous and/or salary requested, year of high school graduation (regardless of your age) and other questions that you may prefer not to answer.

I do not know of any online applications that will allow you to skip a field (i.e.: not supply an answer). In this case, I recommend that you fill out the application honestly and completely.

The only other alternative you have is not to apply.

Email Address

You must have a professional email address. First and Last Name is always best (rick.gillis@... for example). Save your "hotandsexy@ email address for your friends.

Phone Number

Every recruiter in the free-world will tell you that you are wasting your time by placing more than one phone number on your resume. Unless they have reason to believe you are the guy who will cure cancer and generate billions of dollars in revenue, recruiters most often won't call second numbers! This is where young people who generally don't have landlines have it over the older generations. They won't miss that call.

If you maintain a landline, place that phone number on your resume. Then, each time you leave the house — even to run a short errand — forward your landline to your cellphone so you won't miss a call. Don't know how to do that? Google *72 and *73 to learn how to forward and disconnect your phone from the service your phone provider offers.

Relocation/Travel

I told you I want your recruiter to begin to like you from your resume – your first "first impression." The Relocation/Travel entry on your resume is where this likability begins. In this space, you provide information that is useful to the recruiter but does not give away any details. I want them to call you for those. To a recruiter, this knowledge may help move you further along the process more quickly should the position you are seeking call for relocation or travel.

Look at the sample Short-Form Resume and notice that Jerry Job Seeker is "Willing to Relocate/Travel 70%" meaning that Jerry will move for the right position and is willing to travel up to 70% of the month. Of course if you are not able or willing to do, so don't make any such statement.

Also, note that using the term "Willing" implies that you will consider doing so at your own expense. Alternately, stating that you are "Open to Relocation" implies that you are willing to do so if the company covers expenses. Semantics are important in job search!

Telephone Area Code
Yes, I know the Jerry Job Seeker resume says, "Currently residing in Houston, TX" but this is because (1) Jerry did not provide a street address, (2) his phone number listed (in the sample) indicates that he lives in New York City as evidenced by the 212 area code (this is the assumption a recruiter will make) and (3) Jerry is applying for a job in the Houston area. It is important to this scenario that the recruiter know that he is local and available for the job. Jerry just happens to be carrying a "long-distance" cell phone.

This occurs more and more often in cellphone-America. Young people go off to college and obtain a phone number local to their school. Upon returning home, their cell area codes no longer match generally recognized local area codes. This has also become a common occurrence among professionals of all stripes. We are, after all, a highly mobile nation. It is therefore common that a recruiter's first thought would be that an applicant is applying for the job from outside the area. (See Home Address as Disqualifier above for "red line" implications.)

Other Relevant Information

Although the sample resume has "Bilingual (English/Spanish)" as a place holder in this spot, this is the space to note any special skill, expertise or other qualification you might have (i.e.: security clearance, certifications, or even licenses you hold) that could further enhance consideration of your application. Make sure the information you place here has high relevance to the position you seek or the expertise you offer. Otherwise, omit this entry and consider placing it at the bottom of your resume in your Education or Other Information sections.

Non-Smoker

Wow, does this get people riled up! Like them or not, we all know the facts (coming from someone who smoked for I-don't-know-how-many-years): smokers cost companies money in lost production, higher insurance rates, second-hand smoke litigation, etc. The general preference within most companies is to hire non-smokers. (Some companies require employees to sign a non-smoking affidavit that states they may be terminated if violated. So far, this requirement has been upheld in court.) If you do not smoke, state it up front. It's one more reason for them to "like" you early on. This item could be one of those little incidental items that get you consideration over someone else.

• • •

You have now completed the header of your Short-Form Resume. In just an inch or so of space you have provided the recruiter or hiring manager with a large amount of quality information that can push your resume to the top and get you that all-important phone call.

The Seeking Statement—One Line That Can Make All the Difference

> **I am seeking the position of International Sales Manager for Giant Industrial Corporation reference #12345**

Of the thousands of resumes I have reviewed over the years, it would be my guess that no more than 1% actually stated the position the applicants were seeking. This is one of the most consistent faults I find with resumes: I don't know what the job seeker wants to do.

So I created the Seeking Statement, a device that hiring professionals and business owners appreciate. Why? Because it gets right to the point by telling your reader exactly the position you seek. Nothing more, nothing less. But it turns out that this one line of information serves a much broader function than I knew when I first conceived it. More on this in a moment.

> ### Cover Letters: Useful or Useless?
> You might think that submitting a cover letter with your resume would make clear the position you seek (especially if you don't modify your resume for each position you apply to). In most cases you would be wrong. Of the professional recruiters I have questioned regarding cover letters, most all of them have told me they don't even read cover letters. This position is also strongly supported in the HR/recruiting forums I pore over each week.
>
> Some consider the cover letter a "supporting document" and may read them only if the resume makes an impression.
>
> Note, however, that if the job posting states that in order to apply for a position you must "submit your cover letter and resume" *by all means do so*! Even though your cover letter *may not be reviewed*, consider this requirement as the first test by the employer to see if you can follow instructions. In such cases, resumes received without a cover letter are generally dismissed from consideration.

The Seeking Statement centered and in bold type directly below your contact information, states exactly the **title of the position** you are seeking, the **name of the company** and the **reference number**, if there is one, for the position sought. Yes, I know what you are thinking. Why would you include the company name in the Seeking Statement? Doesn't the person receiving the resume know where they are currently employed?

The reason is resume filtering software. In ranking your resume, it may give you a single point (+1) for mentioning the company on your resume, and I know of at least one filtering program that allows 2 points for mentioning the company twice in the body of your scanned resume. (And you want all the points you can get from the grading system—er, software.)

The function of the reference number in your Seeking Statement is to make certain your resume is routed to the correct person in the right department.

How the Federal Government Makes Job Seeking More Difficult and How the Seeking Statement Solves the Problem

Here is why I didn't know how smart I was by creating the Seeking Statement; it serves a much broader function than just announcing the position you desire.

In the first years of the new millennium, the U.S. Department of Labor (DOL), in conjunction with the Society for Human Resource Management (SHRM), determined that minorities were not being well served by online employment technology such as job boards and corporate job sites. As a result and in the interest of diversity hiring, the DOL and specifically the Office of Federal Contract Compliance Programs (OFCCP) issued a rule that took effect February 6, 2006, and remains in effect today, stating that all federal contractors and subcontractors would be required to gather information from all applicants regarding their race, gender and ethnicity. The information is archived and made available to the DOL when requested. This rule impacts the job seeker because the U.S. government, being the single largest purchaser of goods and services in the nation, employs and otherwise contracts with tens of thousands of companies who, in turn, manage subcontractors. You may be applying to these companies for work.

In applying for various positions online, you may have noticed questions related to race, ethnicity and gender. They are generally placed near the end of the application in response to this "Internet Applicant" rule and are used to gather this demographic information should the DOL/OFCCP request it from the employer. From a job seeking point of view, answering these questions is voluntary and will not impact your application. I recommend you provide the information requested but it's your call. This data is not to be used by the organization for hiring purposes and is stored separately from your resume in the event the DOL requires an employer/contractor to support its diversity hiring.

To successfully submit your resume to a company governed by this ruling, it is necessary that you declare "an expression of interest in employment" (see box below). If you do not, the company is not required to consider your resume if you apply by resume –as opposed to using the corporate online application.

The following excerpt is copied directly from the DOL website.

What is the definition of an "Internet Applicant" in the final rule?

An Internet Applicant is defined as an individual who satisfies the following four criteria:

- The individual submits **an expression of interest in employment** through the Internet or related electronic data technologies;
- The contractor considers the individual for employment in a particular position;
- The individual's **expression of interest** indicates the individual possesses the basic qualifications for the position; and,
- The individual at no point in the contractor's selection process prior to receiving an offer of employment from the contractor, removes himself or herself from further consideration or otherwise indicates that he or she is no longer interested in the position.

Source:

www.dol.gov/ofccp/regs/compliance/faqs/iappfaqs.htm#Q6Gl

9/18/11

(This link is subject to change. Search "internet applicant" on the DOL.gov website for most current information.)

How to Declare Expression of Interest

Your Seeking Statement serves the purpose of expressing your interest in this employment opportunity by stating the title of the job you are seeking <u>exactly</u> as it is stated in the posting. To illustrate, this means that if you submit your resume using "Benefits Manager" as the job title while the job posting lists it as "Senior Compensation and Benefits Manager," you may not be considered for the position since you did not technically meet the "expression of interest" criteria. I'm not saying you won't be considered for the job but I am saying that if I were the recruiter assigned to screen the 200 resumes received for this position, I could (legally) look for any reason to reduce the number of resumes I need to plow through.

The Generic Seeking Statement

It's important that you formulate a "generic" Seeking Statement for the resume you keep on your person at all times during your job search. Your generic seeking statement will necessarily be broader in scope than one for a specific employer. For example a salesperson's generic Seeking Statement might read: "I am seeking a Position in Advertising, Sales or Marketing."

Keep in mind that the Seeking Statement must, by virtue of your applying to multiple positions, be changed to reflect each position you apply for. Your generic Seeking Statement is meant for times when you are able to spontaneously hand someone your resume (i.e.: job fairs, corporate open houses, networking events, etc.).

• • •

As simple as such a single sentence might appear to be, the Seeking Statement accomplishes a lot: the recruiter knows exactly what job you are seeking and therefore is more inclined to "like" you, it punches up the score your resume receives from the filtering software and it prevents your resume from possibly being disallowed for lack of an "expression of interest in employment."

The Objective Statement

<u>Objective Statement</u>
As a result of my skills, experience and education I am capable of significantly increasing net revenue by implementation of innovative, proven management, motivational and sales training techniques.

I call most resumes "obituaries" because they speak to the past. The Short-Form Resume speaks to the future and it happens right here in the Objective Statement—a single line that tells the reader what you are going to do for the organization upon being hired. Keep it short. One sentence is all it takes. Keep your audience in mind and state how you will make them money or save them money or, if the position you seek is not a revenue-generating job, how you will add value to the organization or save time by doing the job more efficiently than anyone else can.

A close friend of mine, the Director of Staffing for a national corporation, called me when I was writing one of my previous books and asked what my book was about. In response I asked him, "How many times in your 33 years of interviewing people have you heard someone say that they were there to increase shareholder value?"

He said he had never heard that before whereupon I said, "Bingo, that's why I'm writing this book!"

Now I'm not implying that the position you seek will directly return value to corporate shareholders but the principle remains the same. Look back at my sample Objective Statement and closely examine the phrase "As a result of my skills, experience and education I am capable of…" Now complete that sentence. Regardless of your level of experience you can complete that one line affirmatively. Based on the posting you are applying for, how will you add value to the company? More to the point you may be surprised to know that such a powerful statement is virtually unseen and unspoken in the preliminaries of job search.

Selected Accomplishments

I have already provided you with all the information you need to draft stunning accomplishments and now it's time for you to place your top four most appropriate, personal-best achievements on your Short-Form Resume. Note the title of this section on the sample resume: Selected Accomplishments. I am fond of the word "selected" because it implies that you have many more such accomplishments to discuss with your recruiter—and that requires a phone call on their part.

Selected Accomplishments
- Inherited and then overcame a $5,000,000 deficit in a badly designed national sales promotion by completely redesigning and developing a far superior plan resulting in a new system that reduced typical man hours the sales staff devoted to plan by 23% while increasing sales in excess of $1,000,000 per quarter.
- Saved over $500,000 annually in key sales communication systems and national transportation expenses while improving level of service to clientele.
- Dramatically reduced sales staff turnover by 28% due to more focused recruiting and selection process. Enhanced training and the creation of targeted management groups resulting in countless man-hour savings.
- Analyzed and merged more than 14 compensation plans into one corporate plan that resulted in a savings exceeding $270,000 the following fiscal year while continuing to fairly compensate the sales staff for their efforts.

• • •

After providing relevant, useful information in your Header - a Seeking Statement that clearly states the position you seek, an Objective Statement declaring how you will bring value to the organization, and now an abbreviated list of personal best accomplishments to attest to your value - you have completed the first half of your Short-Form Resume!

Job!

Chapter 6

Short-Form Resume – The Second Half

"Humans are allergic to change. They love to say,
'We've always done it this way.'
I try to fight that. That's why I have a clock on my wall
that runs counter-clockwise."
Grace Hopper

You have completed the first half of your Short-Form Resume by providing information a potential employer wants to see and hear. The top half sets the hook, if you will – it gains immediate attention.

The information necessary to complete your Short-Form Resume, excluding keywords, can most likely be taken directly from your existing resume. But like everything else I have presented to you up to this point, you need to make some changes for each entry. Here is a sample:

Employment History

<u>**Employment History**</u>
Giant National Employment Website, Atlanta, GA   Jan 2002 – Jan 2010
      Director, West Coast Sales
Giant National Employment Website is recognized as the world's leading employment website.
Gulf Coast Group Internet, Houston, TX   1998 - 2001
      Sales Manager, South Central US
Texas based Gulf Coast Group is one of the nation's leading providers of employment technology solutions offering full-service employment management systems as well as social media expertise.
The Express Internet Company, New Orleans, LA   1997 – 1998
      Employment Internet Startup Consultant
The Express Internet Company, operating primarily in the Southeastern US, offers turnkey Internet services from web design to network applications.

The first thing to notice about the Employment History section of the Short-Form Resume is that each entry is ideally, only four lines long. This is by design. For reasons stated previously, you know the objective is to keep this document to a single page while making sure it grabs your reader's attention.

In the sample above, notice that each employment listing is composed of 3 elements.

1. Company Name, Location, Dates of Employment
The first line of Jerry Job Seeker's most recent employment entry begins with the Company Name (Giant National Employment Website) followed by location (Atlanta, GA) and his Dates of Employment (Jan 2002-Present). These are the <u>only</u> dates you will use on your Short-Form Resume! (More about dates later.)

2. Your Job Title
The next line in your employment entry is for your Job Title.

3. **A Single Line About the Company (Not You)**

I call this line the "About Us" line because this information can usually be found on the company's website under the About Us button or, quite often, you can use the first line taken from a corporate website's homepage. Those marketing folks worked hard to state clearly and succinctly what the company does or stands for. Take advantage of their hard work. The sole purpose of this line on your resume is to identify the *company that employed you* as opposed to a conventional resume where at this point you would begin singing your praises, your responsibilities, etc. which you already did in your Selected Accomplishments.

This is a switch on the traditional resume that saves space and works well. And, regardless of the name recognition factor of your previous employer (say, for example, you worked for Microsoft), provide this one line about the company. Do not assume that everyone knows who Microsoft is.

Let's try one to show you how I would locate the one line about the company. Let's assume that your last position had been with American Express. Looking on AmericanExpress.com, I found the following sentence on the About American Express page.

> *"American Express is a global services company, providing access to products, insights and experiences that enrich lives and build business success."*

Who better than American Express to describe what they do? You, as a former employee building your resume, can use this statement to identify your former employer.

After completing your first entry, continue adding previous employers in reverse chronological order (most recent at the top). In the interest of minimizing age discrimination, I recommend that you list an employment history not to exceed more than 25 to 28 years.

Yes, omitting earlier employment might be a little white lie but I have a couple of reasons for suggesting this. One, although some job search experts recommend that you list no more than 10 years of employment history on your resume, if you show up at an interview with only a decade on your resume and as much gray hair as I have, everything you say from "nice to meet you" forward will be suspect.

Second, there is often a good chance that what you were doing professionally 25-plus years ago has little value in your current job search discussion.

I Didn't Work for a Recognized Company

If you worked for an organization that does not maintain a website, look at the sample resume and try to emulate the one-line descriptions I created. The concept remains the same: one line to describe the company mission. This is not about you.

I Spent My Entire Career with a Single Company

If you spent your career climbing only one corporate ladder, you might be wondering how to handle the one-line employment history entry. No problem. Prepare the entry as you would if you had worked at other companies but instead of moving on to entries 2 and 3, list your most recent position held followed by the position/job title you held prior to that and so on. For example:

ABCD Company, Portland, OR   May 1977—Sep 2011
    Senior Vice President, Sales   Mar 2003—Sep 2011
ABCD Company is a nationally recognized leader in the development and management of corporate office park communities with 26 properties located in 23 cities across the US.
    Division Manager, Sales & Marketing   Dec 1996—Mar 2003
    Field Sales National Director   Jul 1985—Dec 1996
Promotion based on attainment of highest rental rate/square foot for 3 consecutive years.
    General Manager, San Antonio, TX   Aug 1979—Jul 1985
    Leasing Manager, San Antonio, TX   May 1977—Aug 1979

Should this format leave significant white space on your resume, you may want to place filler comments between entries such as the notation following the Field Sales National Manager *position listed above. Be certain details you state here are not just re-assertions of your Selected Accomplishments.*

Skeptical?

I understand you might be skeptical about my abbreviated employment history format but doing the same thing over and over while expecting a different result is, as Albert Einstein said, crazy. So if what you have been doing hasn't been working, maybe it's time to try a different approach.

Education, Awards, Honors, Other Relevant Information

Bachelor of Science Management, Park University, Parkville, MO
Veteran USAF, Honorable Discharge
Member, Board of Directors, Ronald McDonald House

Once again, take a look at the sample Short-Form Resume. Did you notice there is no header for Education? This is another of those it's-always-been-that-way-so-I-will-too kinds of wasted space. Isn't it obvious to a recruiter when they see "Bachelor of Science Management, Park University" or "MBA, Georgetown University" that they will figure out that this entry reflects education? Keep in mind that it is in your interest to save valuable real estate (space) on the page. The time will come shortly when you will need it.

The Mock Education Listing

If you did not obtain a degree but have some college courses under your belt, you are better off NOT listing the college you attended. On resumes, placing college references infers that you graduated. I once counseled a job seeker who had such a listing on his resume but written in a manner that I was not certain if he had, in fact, received his college degree. So I asked him if he had graduated. Note that this is a yes or no question. He told me that he was "only six hours short of his degree" which meant that he did not hold a college degree. So then the question becomes what else is he not telling us? In this case, it is actually better to say, "attended such and such college" and then be prepared to explain why you did not graduate. Recruiters and hiring managers recognize that "life happens."

It's worth repeating: do not lie or misrepresent yourself on your resume. Recruiters are looking for such misstatements and with Google, social media and background services available today, it's easier than ever to determine if someone is lying.

But You Have Enough Life Experience to Justify a College Degree
Several years back Jack Welch, the former CEO of GE and his wife, Suzy, used to write, "The Welch Way," a Q & A column in Business Week magazine. One of my favorites was when a reader asked whether a degree from an Ivy League school was worth more than a degree from a state university. Mr. Welch's answer was short and to the point: your undergraduate degree is good for 30 days. He went on to say that he would know within 30 days whether or not you could do the job regardless of where you had obtained your degree.

I have taken that answer and created a spin for job seekers I work with who have considerable life experience but no formal education. If this is your situation, I encourage you to create and format your Short-Form Resume in the manner you have learned up to now but when you arrive at what would be the education section, skip it.

Even without education being listed, because you have done a bang-up job on your Selected Accomplishments, the recruiter who reviews your resume is still going to call. But you can expect a question others may not hear: "I don't see any education listed…"

In response, you can say that, "According to Jack Welch - you know, the former CEO of GE - an undergraduate degree is only good for 30 days and you can bet that within my first 30 days with your company, you will see the value I bring as a result of my professional experience."

I admit that not everyone has the cheek to pull off this kind of declaration but if education is a requirement, a recruiter has to ask the question and if you don't have the diploma what have you got to lose? By the way, this answer really works well in the on-site interview where you can add professional "posturing" to your answer.

A Note Regarding the Community Service Listing

You will notice that I have added an entry to indicate that Jerry Job Seeker is a member of the Board of Directors of Ronald McDonald House. I placed this here to provoke some thought on your part. In some cases, this listing may be seen as a good thing—networking and your involvement in the community. But I have seen some resumes with so many community group listings that I have to wonder if time spent on the candidate's outside activities would impact their time on the job. You might also keep this suggestion in mind when creating your Accomplishments Statement. Too many community service entries can actually work against you. Always keep your audience in mind.

· · ·

Congratulations! With the exception of the final—and maybe most important section of your resume: Keywords (which is a purely "mechanical" process), you have completed your Short-Form Resume! I promised that you would be able to use the Short-Form Resume to apply for virtually every job you are qualified for. Here is how.

Print and review your newly completed resume and notice that the changes necessary to customize it for each position you apply for are (1) the Seeking Statement, (2) the Objective Statement, and (3) you may wish to leave your Selected Accomplishments as they are or you might decide to choose others from your list that are more relevant to a given job listing.

For now that's it except—and this is an important exception — for the addition of strategic keywords which you will learn all about in the next chapter.

Job!

Chapter 7

Keywords

"You have to put in many, many, many tiny efforts that nobody sees or appreciates before you achieve anything worthwhile."
Brian Tracy

You may wonder why I devote an entire chapter just to the keywords portion of your Short-Form Resume. Instead of answering that question, let me ask another.

How many times have you submitted your resume to a job posting that you matched your qualifications to a "T" and never heard a word back from the company?

By the end of this chapter you will have the answers to both questions – yours and mine - and you will be astonished at how simple those answers are. Hint: it involves recruiters' widespread use of resume filtering software which I alluded to earlier and will now explain.

In a Nutshell

The need for HR software management tools came about due to the overwhelming response by job seekers to online job postings. This is not good and it's not bad. It is what it is and in order to successfully navigate the minefield that is electronic resume submission, you must know and understand this conceptually simple system. It will help you to find and use the right keywords in job postings if you understand how resume filtering software works.

It is rare these days when you hit the send button, that your resume or online application lands in the inbox of a real, human person. Instead, it is sent, with all the other resumes received for the same position, into a dark hole known as a database where it sits untouched by human hands, unread, unnoticed.

Then, when it is time for the hiring manager to sift through the resumes, he or she taps into this database using the key terms and phrases contained in the job posting. The software retrieves only those resumes that include most if not all of the terms—keywords— found in that posting. Essentially you need to remember that as much as possible, your resume must "mirror" the job posting's terminology.

The more terms your resume contains that are in the job posting, the higher your "grade" and the more likely your resume will receive consideration.

So, keywords are the "safety net" (the last section of your resume) that will promote your visibility to the professional recruiter. You must include them in your resume or it may be lost forever in that deep, dark hole–the database.

Right now, I'm betting that you are already trying to figure out how to plant all the correct keywords and phrases without having to create a separate resume for each posting. Not so fast.

First, some basic homework on keywords will make it easy for you to use them effectively in your job search.

What Are Keywords, Key Terms, or Key Phrases?

Keywords are certain words and phrases that give a job posting definition. For example, when you see an ad stating, "Candidate must possess a high level of proficiency in Microsoft Office," there you have it: 'Microsoft Office' is the key phrase, right?

Well, that's only part of it. "Microsoft Office" alone is not as likely to get your resume to pop up out of the database because the phrase "high level of proficiency" enhances the definition of the job posting by stating the level of experience required for the position.

So the phrase for your keyword list would be: "high level proficiency Microsoft Office." Without the experience depiction you could lose your chance at an interview.

But before we get into more details of matching keywords in the job posting, you need a list of keywords that apply to your industry - keywords you will use on every resume you submit no matter what the job posting states.

The Lingo of Your Industry

The lingo of your industry is the basis or starting point for your permanent list of generic keywords—that is, the jargon, terminology and phrases you would use among your peers on the job.

Begin your generic keyword list by working from memory. Jot down those terms you would use with coworkers talking shop over a cup of coffee. Then start reviewing job postings, industry websites, white papers and other related trade publications and add to your list those terms you notice that you can professionally speak to.

Do not choose keywords you do not fully comprehend. If you don't know "ERP" (Enterprise Resource Planning software) for example, don't suggest that you do by placing it in your keywords.

Continue to create this list over time but for now, let's get back to keywords in the job posting.

Job Posting Keywords

Filtering software doesn't just store resumes to be retrieved later by the hiring manager. Among other features it also provides the recruiter with a template for the job posting. To show you how it works, let's pretend I am a manager who needs to hire an administrative assistant. Here is how the creation of the modern job posting happens.

I send an email to HR asking them to post a job for me that include the following 10 qualities, skills and conditions that my ideal candidate will have.

1. Administrative Assistant
2. 3 Years Experience Minimum
3. Located in Houston, TX
4. College Degree Preferred
5. Bilingual (English/Spanish) Preferred
6. Microsoft Office (Word, Excel, PowerPoint) Proficient
7. Quicken Proficient
8. Contribute Proficient
9. Professional Demeanor
10. Accounting Experience a Bonus

Here is what the ad HR creates would look like.

Giant Staffing Company

Administrative Assistant Position

Post Date: Current   Type: Full time

Start Date: Salary: Open

Location: Houston   Job Reference: #12345

Job Description:

Giant's Clerical, Administrative, Legal & Professional Division is currently seeking a professional, experienced Administrative Assistant to work with our clients throughout the Southwest Houston area. Qualified candidate will have a minimum of 3 years' experience working in an administrative capacity in a corporate environment. Bilingual skills (English/Spanish) are preferred. The right candidate will maintain a professional demeanor, be articulate, have strong attention to detail (such as name pronunciation and spelling), and must be able to multi-task. Chosen candidate will have a very professional appearance and strong business etiquette. A college degree is preferred but not necessarily required. Candidate will be proficient in MS Office (Word, Excel, PowerPoint), Quicken and Macromedia Contribute software. Accounting experience is a bonus! Salary range: $18-25/hr DOE.

Now, since you are seeking an administrative position, you decide to apply for this job using your Short-Form Resume.

Your task is to identify the keywords in the previous posting and add them to the list of generic keywords at the bottom of your Short-Form Resume. Remember that your objective is to suitably impress the scanning software (not me—not yet anyway) by matching the terminology in the posting.

Here is the ad again with the keywords necessary to get my attention in bold:

Giant Staffing Company*
Administrative Assistant Position*

Post Date: Current	Type: **Full time**
Start Date:	Salary: Open
Location: **Houston**	Job Reference: #**12345***

Job Description:

Giant's **Clerical**, **Administrative**, **Legal** & **Professional** Division is currently seeking a professional, **experienced** Administrative Assistant to work with our clients throughout the **Southwest Houston** area. Qualified candidate will have a minimum of **3 years' experience** working in an administrative capacity in a **corporate environment**. **Bilingual** skills (**English/Spanish**) are preferred. The right candidate will maintain a **professional demeanor**, be **articulate**, have **strong attention to detail** (such as **name pronunciation** and **spelling**), and must be able to **multi-task**. Chosen candidate will have a **professional appearance** and **strong business etiquette**. A **college degree** is preferred but not necessarily required. Candidate will be **proficient in MS Office** (**Word, Excel, PowerPoint**), **Quicken** and **Macromedia Contribute** software. **Accounting experience** is a bonus!
Salary range: $18-25/hr DOE.

I placed an asterisk next to the Company Name, the Position Title and the Reference Number. Those terms should already appear in your

Seeking Statement so there is no need to repeat them in your keywords section (although doing so will not hurt).

Also note that any terms in your generic (never-to-be-removed) keywords do not need to be repeated.

Taken as a whole, here is what the keywords from this job posting would look like on your Short-Form Resume:

> **Keywords:** full time Houston clerical administrative legal professional experienced Southwest Houston 3 years' experience corporate environment bilingual English Spanish professional demeanor articulate strong attention to detail name pronunciation spelling multi-task professional appearance strong business etiquette college degree proficient in MS Office Word Excel PowerPoint Quicken Macromedia Contribute accounting experience

You would then add these terms to the generic list of key terms you have already created.

The Process Continued

Here is what happens at Giant Staffing Company a week after the job is posted.

HR tells me that my posting received 3,223 resumes. This, unfortunately, is not an unusual number of responses to a position of this type posted for an entire week by a national firm which demonstrates exactly why you need to understand and use keywords.

No manager, certainly not me, has time or the desire to review 3,223 resumes. I ask if HR can remove from consideration all those resumes that do not have at least 9 of my 10 original qualities, skills and conditions I require or prefer of my ideal candidate.

That reduces the number to 723 resumes – those having at least 9 items from my original 'wish list.'

This is crazy! I don't have time to review 723 resumes! So once again I ask HR to run a second scan and give me only those resumes that have all 10 items from my list PLUS those requirements that enhanced my posting that HR traditionally adds to virtually all postings ("attention to detail", "professional appearance", "strong business etiquette," etc.).

How many resumes made the final cut? 12!

Of 3,223 resumes received, 3,211 will get no consideration whatever! They will never be seen by a real, human person simply because they did not know what you now know about keywords.

This is why I say that job search is no longer about selection but about preventing elimination.

• • •

Placement of Your Keywords on Your Short-Form Resume
There is a simple protocol to the placement of keywords on your resume. There is no need for punctuation or columns. Review the Short-Form Resume sample and notice that each term is placed, a space is skipped and the next word or phrase is added.

Since this document is principally designed to be used online, a 4 to 6 point font is good. Yes, that's very small type but the keywords are for the benefit of the scanning software, not for a person to read.

Once you have added keywords from the job posting, your work is done - your resume is good to go.

All the above can be applied to an online application as well. Seek out the terms posted and be certain that they land somewhere in the app—any field with extra blank space will do—before you hit Enter.

For resumes you will take to job fairs or networking events, increase the keyword font size to 8 points. This is important because a recruiter will scan your resume into a corporate database (you didn't think they save all those paper resumes did you?) using Optical Character Recognition software (OCR) and anything smaller than 8 points may not be legible to the OCR which may render your keywords useless.

Conclusion

Obviously, you must check your keywords against every job posting you respond to and match them. In all likelihood, the terms you extract from one posting will work for other jobs too. And as you add to your list of keywords, more and more of them will become "generic" and therefore valuable for permanent retention.

You may think that you might be placing too many words in the Keyword section of your Short-Form Resume. I have successfully worked with clients who have inserted upwards of 600 terms in their Keywords section using single spacing and a 4 point font. (For reference, this paragraph contains 54 words including this sentence.)

• • •

So, as you can see, the keyword section of your Short-Form Resume is always a work in progress, and now you know the answer to both of those questions at the start of this chapter: keywords, keywords, keywords.

They are most likely the reason no one responded to the resume you submitted for that job that fit you to a "T"— you simply didn't make the cut because you didn't know how to play the game. Keyword inclusion in your resume is crucial to your job search—that's why I spent an entire chapter on them.

Now it's time to get your resume, with all the necessary keywords, into the hands of those people currently seeking you and your skill set.

Job!

Chapter 8

The Long-Form (or Traditional) Resume

"Experience is not what happens to a man.
It is what a man does with what happens to him."
Aldous Huxley

Let me set the scene for you. You submit your Short-Form Resume for a position and you get the call I warned you about—the one from a recruiter telling you that she received your resume and while she finds it compelling, she needs more information. You respond by telling her that you submitted your Short-Form (or an Abbreviated) Resume in order to get her attention and that you are prepared to send over your Long-Form (or Traditional) Resume on the spot. All you need is her email address.

In order for that to happen you need to have that traditional resume ready to launch. Let's wrap up this process and knock out your Long-Form Resume so it will be ready to go. After everything you have learned up to now, this will be a snap.

• • •

Welcome to the Long-Form Resume

The Short-Form Resume is not meant to be your sole job seeking tool. It is intended to be step 2 of my 3 step job search process. The third step is the creation of a thought-provoking, accomplishments-based, Long-Form Resume and you now have a choice to make:

- You can take your original, "obituary" resume and enhance it based on what you have learned up to this point (accomplishments, accomplishments, accomplishments), or
- You can take your marvel of a Short-Form Resume and expand the Employment History section for your Long Form Resume by going into greater detail.

Option 1: Polishing the Old Obituary

Let's start with the first option—improving the resume you brought to the table when you first began this book. Review it to determine what no-brainer changes you can make based on what you've learned so far: remove your physical address, add a Seeking Statement and repeatedly stress the value you bring to an organization.

The most crucial part of polishing your existing resume remains the requirement that net results be stated with each claimed achievement. If you said you purchased and implemented $3,000,000 worth of software, declare the impact of that purchase on the company as you learned in Chapter 3.

Option 2: Expanding the Employment History Section of the Short-Form Resume

By far, the better option—especially after all the time you have invested in this process—is to apply the Short-Form Resume format to your new Long-Form.

There is good chance the hiring manager and others have seen your Short-Form Resume prior to your arrival. Why change horses in the middle of the stream? Additionally, the Objective Statement and Selected Accomplishments from the Short-form resume convey your value while quietly setting the stage for presentation of your comprehensive Accomplishments Statement.

I'm willing to bet you can easily enhance the Employment History section in the Long-Form Resume by extracting whole segments from your existing resume and pasting them into your new Long-Form Resume making certain to modify them as necessary to state the net outcome.

In the event you decide to write new copy for the Employment History section, you can use former job descriptions as a launching point. State your responsibilities and then fill in the blanks with the priceless information you compiled on your Accomplishments Statement.

There is nothing wrong with restating that information in your Long-Form Resume – in fact, you should do so for persons further up the line who may not receive a copy of your Short-Form Resume.

Length of the Long-Form Resume

The length of your new Long-From Resume is up to you—within reason.

The length is not as important as the information it contains because you know that a real, human person will be reviewing it. With the Short-Form Resume, we were concerned with software protocols. No more.

That said, don't make it too long. Two pages are great. Three are good. Four or five might be OK if you have a compelling message. My best advice is to save some of it for the interview.

One last note—don't forget to add page numbers and your name to each page of the Long-Form Resume. This is the one time you have my permission to use the header/footer function of your document software.

Sample Long-Form Resume Created on the Short-Form Model

The resume sample that follows was provided to me for review by a client. He had done such a good job of taking the Short-Form Resume model and enhancing it through the addition of responsibilities and accomplishments that after removing any identifying information I present it here for your review. Professionally printed this document fills the better part of three pages.

Keywords on the Long-Form Resume

Notice that there is not a Keywords section anywhere on this document. However, in a change of opinion from the previous edition of "JOB!", I am now of the opinion that should you determine that additional keywords may serve you well why not do so? I see no problem with you adding any terms or phrases not previously listed on these three pages. Add this Keywords section to the end of the Long-Form Resume—not to the first page.

Sample Long-Form Resume (3 pages)
Jenny Job Seeker

123-456-7890
Willing to travel 50%
Bilingual (Spanish)

jennyjobseeker@email
Currently residing Cleveland, OH
Non-smoker

I am seeking a position with HPS.

Objective Statement

As a result of my skills, experience and education I am capable of being a long-term member of your team by providing empathic support for pet owners, enhancing relationships with clients, and improving efficiency in documentation and communication.

Selected Accomplishments

- As a service writer at Atwater's, I carefully considered the owner's needs, desires, safety, budget, and equipment condition leading to the highest average repair invoices and being the most requested employee in the service department
- Completed over 150 hours in a clinical counseling internship at Island Seminary resulting in consistently positive reviews from my clinical supervisor based upon collaboration with other trainees, client case notes, treatment plans, clinical skills and the ability to develop client rapport
- Established strong customer relationships at TMO resulting in repeat sales and service requests leading to an increase in profits every year, both in product and service, resulting in a significant store expansion in 2007
- Trained employees of 6 different bicycle shops in effective selling of service which resulted in: raising the average invoice amount, improving communication skills, increasing attention to detail, and gaining empathy for the customer's situation

Employment History

SGW School, Liberty, Ohio   August 2012-Present

After Care Coordinator, Extended Care Assistant Teacher, & Substitute Teacher

SGW is a non-profit, non-discriminatory educational organization, welcoming children from preschool through grade eight of all races, religions and national origins.

- Provide structure and care for up to 60 students for up 3 hours after the school day
- Ohio Department of Education Student Aide certified and first aid certified
- Assisted in leading a class of 8 preschool and kindergarteners in a sit down meal and structured afternoon of activities

Atwater's Bike Shop, Akron, Ohio   2003-2004 & 2008-2012

Service Manager

Ohio's oldest and best known bicycle shop has four locations throughout Ohio, and has served their customers with the best in bicycle sales and service since 1940.

- Managed the work of 10 service staff at one of the largest volume bicycle shops in the country, leading to the assembly, service and tuning of over 10,000 bikes per year
- Developed and organized a used bicycle and parts system that went from selling $1,000 of used bicycles to revenue of over $15,000 in bicycles and $3,000 in parts per year
- Converted and retrained a paper-based service department to a fully computer-based system resulting in less paper work along with more accurate estimates, work process scheduling, invoices, inventory, and customer history
- Created employee training and quality control documents leading to over 100 pages of original material

- Proved to be a well-rounded and helpful worker leading to roles as: manager, salesperson, cashier, mechanic, service writer, bicycle fitter, warehouse staff, inventory processor, warranty specialist, new parts buyer, janitor, equipment deliverer, employee trainer and bicycle shop customer service consultant

River Consulting, Cuyahoga Falls, Ohio   2009
Freelance HME Manual Editor
River Consulting offers full service consulting that provides accreditation preparation services for Home Medical Equipment (HME), home health organizations seeking accreditation, and compliance with applicable regulations.

- Edited home medical companies' compliancy, policy and procedure manuals, including creating original customized policies, ensuring ability for Medicare funding
- Assembled professional paper hardcopy and computer-based manuals for each contracted company

Technical Multisport Operations, Columbus, Ohio   2005-2008
Service Manager and Assistant Store Manager
TMO is a professional bicycle and triathlon retail store, providing a niche product line, excellent customer support, and attract demanding, educated customers.

- Contributed to the realized increase in profits every year, both in product and service, resulting in a significant store expansion in 2007
- Established strong customer relationships resulting in repeat sales and service requests leading to be contracted as the first-ever salaried manager in 20 years of operation
- Created a successful customer loyalty program to attract and retain customers resulting in its continued use for almost 10 years
- Provided consultation to small business ownership, which improved efficiency, profitability, and the level of customer service

Spring Ministry Life Center, Cleveland, Ohio   2006
Pastoral Counseling Intern and Volunteer
Spring Ministry staff and volunteers connect with at-risk teens to share God's truth and to equip them with the tools to experience real life change.

- Built trusting relationships with youth in need
- Led activities and games, mentored junior high and senior high students, led Bible studies, and transported students safely to and from their homes
- Created an organizational system for inventory and usage of the center's computer lab

Coastal Counseling, Columbus, Ohio   2005
Counselor Trainee
Through our more than 40 counselors, coaches, and masters student interns we are able to make professionally trained, biblically sound counseling and coaching affordable.

- Diagnosed personal and mental difficulties, created treatment plans, and counseled children and adults, while under supervision
- Collaborated with other trainees in their diagnoses and treatment plans during supervisory meetings
- Treated difficulties such as: anger management, anxiety, attention deficit disorder, depression, family trauma, and substance abuse

Minsk International School, Minsk, Belarus   2001-2002
Science and Mathematics Educator
MIS is a private non-profit institution that offers high quality education in the English language for students from three years through eighteen years of age.

- Planned and taught 7 classes a day in science and mathematics to children ages 5-16 at a school for international students
- Held parent-teacher conferences to inform parents of their children's academic progress and advise them on any need for further assistance
- Served as the lead administrator for two weeks during the school director's absence, and successfully navigated a conflict between a parent and the school

Major University, Canton, Ohio   1999-2000
Co-Student Activities Council Director
Major's S.A.C. creates and promotes campus environments that result in multiple opportunities for student learning and development
- Budgeted, planned, promoted and supervised the social activities of a college campus of 2,000 students
- Increased the number of student volunteers in my committee three-fold in a one-year period
- Delegated to as many as fifty people at a time leading to the successful hosting of two 500 seat dinner events
- Became the top educational technology student resulting in being chosen by the Major College Education Department staff to be a teacher's assistant for a computer and technology training course, with special focus in Microsoft Office and website creation

Education History
Master of Arts in Counseling, Island Theological Seminary, Youngstown, Ohio
Bachelor of Arts in Liberal Arts, Major University, Canton, Ohio

• • •

Job!

Chapter 9

Social Media, LinkedIn and Job Search

"LinkedIn is for the people you know.
Facebook is for the people you used to know.
Twitter is for people you want to know."
Unknown

With new online tools and apps appearing daily in support of job search I run the risk that what I say today could be inaccurate tomorrow. It is safe to say, however, that the work you have done on your resume, keywords and accomplishments up to this point are vital for the successful utilization of social media in your job search.

Forethought and Planning
With social media, as in social networking, you are not looking for a job per se. You are looking for a person who can make a job happen. The question

you have to answer with regard to social media in your job search lies in where you want to direct a contact after that connection is made.

Now and into the future it is inevitable that more companies will accept job search material (notice I did not say resume or application) via a link to your online presence.

This is where forethought and strategic planning on your part becomes necessary. You now have the opportunity to shape and color your message far beyond that of a black and white resume. You can be seen as you want to be seen. You can now provide work samples, illustrations, photographs, video, publications, industry expertise and opinions for an employer to view.

Your job right now (pun intended), if you do not already have a social media presence, is to establish one. For my young readers this is a no-brainer. This is your lifestyle and a major form of communication. For others who have held back on dabbling in social media it's time that you establish a LinkedIn profile at minimum.

Since Facebook, Twitter, Google+ and other such platforms require time to build a comprehensive profile it's a good thing that it takes a day or less to establish a professional Linkedin profile—currently the most widely used tool of choice for recruiters. And the price is right: it's free.

LinkedIn

In no small part and due to the popularity of LinkedIn and the ability for the company to interface with corporate applicant tracking systems I am seeing more companies that will accept a LinkedIn profile link in lieu of a resume.

Creating a Profile

As I mentioned previously you have already done all the work necessary to build a great LinkedIn profile. It resides in the form of your Short-Form Resume. Should you prefer to provide more information go with your Long-Form.

Linkedin offers premium job search features you may want to explore but for the purpose of this discussion I'll leave that up to you to explore on your own.

One thing I like about LinkedIn is that they are not going to ask for any personal information beyond your email address and your ZIP code— and your email address won't be made public unless you choose to do so. That said, at least while in job search mode, I recommend that you provide your email address and a phone number on your profile so that any interested parties are able to reach you quickly. You can always remove this information later.

After completing the profile add a professional headshot (a good selfie will work just fine), obtain a minimum of three recommendations from co-workers, supervisors or professors and you are in business.

Why am I spending so much time here 'promoting' LinkedIn? Well, personally I am very active on LinkedIn and working with job search clients I know how they get found. More to the point LinkedIn is the first place recruiters go when seeking a candidate to fill a position and it is the site a recruiter or hiring manager will search you out on after receiving your resume submitted via any other application process.

Keywords and LinkedIn

In Chapter 7 you learned about the application of Keywords in your resume. Everything you learned in that chapter applies to your LinkedIn profile as well because every word and phrase in your profile is searchable.

If you decide to add keywords to enhance your searchability consider placing them in the *Specialties* section of your LinkedIn *Summary*.

As an example visit my profile on LinkedIn (https://www.linkedin.com/in/rickgillis). At the bottom of the *Background/Summary* and just above the video players you will see a section called *Specialties*. At the end of this section and to serve this illustration I have placed the phrase 'age discrimination.' This key phrase is something I can talk to as I'm an expert on the topic as it relates to job search but it does not particularly fit into any of the descriptions of my employment history you see further down the page. Therefore I placed it in *Specialties* so that I would be found should anyone search LinkedIn for an individual using the phrases 'job search' and 'age discrimination.'

• • •

Don't be afraid of making mistakes on LinkedIn. If you don't like the way your profile looks or reads all you have to do is go back, click EDIT and make the change. If you are new to LinkedIn I suggest that you seek out the profiles of individuals who do what you do and emulate what you most like about their profile. LinkedIn is user friendly and as a result globally popular.

I recommend that you utilize all the tools that LinkedIn offers. You might want to visit YouTube and check out various 'how-to' videos if you are so inclined.

Other Social Media

LinkedIn is obviously not the only game in town but as of today LinkedIn by far outpaces any other website when it comes to job search.

Media platforms such as Twitter, Facebook, Google+ and <u>YouTube</u> are also viable job search tools. Rather than go into detail explaining the ups and downs, ins and outs of job search on these websites I recommend that you investigate each in your own time and determine which, if any will best serve your needs. All you need to do to get current information on any site you may be interested in learning more about is to Google "YouTube (or whatever site or app) and job search."

Apps

You will also want to look at job search apps. There are dozens! Some are really good while others are good but only regional in capability (i.e.: Silicon Valley, NYC, etc.). Others are industry specific and still others are mini-versions of previously mentioned sites or job boards. Everybody is in the job search space or soon will be due to the capacity for job search to generate revenue where nothing else will. This tends to lead to a 'flavor of the month' effect with some good ideas going away quickly and some others that should die sooner than later surviving due to their ability to attract venture capital. As long as they are free why not try them out? Read the reviews for those that charge a fee before pursuing.

Your Website and Blog

One of the best professional investments you can make in yourself lies in creating a professional website or blog. You should come up with and register a domain name for each but it is not absolutely necessary for a blog. Both take a lot of time with the website requiring much more effort. A blog does not take as much effort to create thanks to hosting services like WordPress and Blogger among others.

The trick to a personal website is not to make it a landing space for pictures of the family vacation, fishing photos and golf outings. After you land your next position do as you like with your site but for the purpose of job search I recommend that you go with only 4 or 5 pages and use each to feature your resume, accomplishments, bio, charitable or volunteer activities and another page to focus on awards, honors and maybe publications. The content will depend very much on what you do or aspire to do. A musicologist would have a site laid out much differently than, say, an electrical engineer. Once again review sites that you admire and emulate.

A blog on the other hand can be a place where you post professional opinions on your industry as well as a personal website supporting all that you offer an employer. Once again this is far too deep a topic for much more than this short examination on the topic but you can investigate both to determine if either is a viable alternative for what you may want to present to the hiring public.

Job!

Chapter 10

Additional Thoughts on This Job Search Thing

*"It's not who you know. It's not even what you know.
It's who knows what you know that makes a career."*
Unknown

Thank You Cards

I want to present you with my number one, crush-the-competition, impress-your-future-employer job search tactic that I insist my clients do upon completion of their interview regardless of the seniority of the position sought: Thank You cards written *on premises*.

In my opinion same-day email Thank You notes are not elegant and a snail mail letter will arrive after the final decision has been made making the effort useless.

The on-premises Thank You card is such a powerful tactic that it has the ability to set you apart from the competition within a few minutes of your departure. My clients carry 10 to 20 blank 4 "x 5" panel cards (available very inexpensively at any box store) with them to the interview and upon completion of the interview return to the lobby or settle into their car and write a thank you note to each person they met during their interview. (Make certain you spell their names correctly!) The reason I recommend you carry so many cards is because you will throw away 2 for every 3 you manage to complete.

Keep the content short. All you have to say is 1) Thank you for your time and interest, 2) I am the perfect person for the position and 3) I look forward to hearing from you soon. If you have job search business cards (see below) toss a couple in before sealing the envelope.

After you have written a similar-but-different note to each person you met during the interview process hand deliver these notes to the receptionist with the request that they be delivered ASAP to the person(s) you just interviewed with.

Have I not told you all along that at the end of the day I want you to be the most compelling and memorable candidate?

Oh, the Clichés'!
Go online and Google "job search clichés." No, really. Do it right now. Scroll down the page a little bit. I'll wait for you.

Did you happen to notice such resume gems as "go-to person," "self-starter," or "problem solver"? How many of these clichés are you currently using?

Understand that it's not the thought behind these overused phrases that bugs recruiters but more the fact that job seekers can't be more original, perhaps even inspired, while stating what they have accomplished in their careers. Hiring managers are seeking people capable of innovative thinking. If you have "good communication skills," here's your chance to express them.

Let me put another resume-filtering software worry into you. Some programs actually have a script that searches those top 100 or so resumes that made the initial keyword cut for just such clichés. The result of this secondary scan is to search for such timeless job search gems as "goal oriented," "results driven" and "team player." Too many of these terms in your resume can actually push your resume back down the rankings.

On the Other Hand
To be fair, you may find yourself required to place such phrases as "team player" in your keywords section. Why? Because not all recruiters take their own advice. They may say they don't care for job search clichés but they themselves often use the very terms they don't care for in their own postings. If it's in the posting, it's a keyword/key phrase.

60-80% of All Jobs Are Found as a Result of Networking
Someone told me this a long time ago and although I have no hard metrics on which to base this statement, I believe it. Your job during job search is to let as many people as possible know that you are in the market. There is no shame in doing so—so do it! (See Job Search Business Cards below for an easy way to accomplish this task.)

When job openings happen at the plant/office/restaurant/retail store/construction site, invariably someone knows someone who would be "perfect for that job." That, in essence, is how networking works. And if you have haven't done the necessary legwork letting everyone know you are available, your name will not be the one brought up as part of the discussion.

Realize that job search really IS all about who you know OR who you want to know. The best way to make this happen is to let not just friends and family, but also your banker, your grocer, your mechanic, your dentist, your accountant—everyone you come in contact with on a daily basis—know that you are "seeking a new opportunity."

Note on **'Seeking a New Opportunity'**
OR
The Importance of Semantics in Job Search

You are not "looking for a job." You are never "looking for a job." You are "seeking a new opportunity"—which to anyone with the authority to hire does not sound desperate. Remember: no one is going to hire your problems.

Nevertheless, and regardless of how much and how hard you network, you must be prepared to deal with the result of successful networking when you get that first phone call from someone interested in discussing an opportunity with you. The steps you have learned up to now—particularly your personal best accomplishments—will serve you well at this point.

Persistence

"Nothing in the world can take the place of persistence:
Talent will not—nothing is more common than unsuccessful men with talent.

Genius will not—unrewarded genius is almost a proverb. Education will not—the world is full of educated failures. Persistence and determination alone are omnipotent."

–President Calvin Coolidge

Thank you President Coolidge. I can't say it any better, so I won't try.

No One is Entitled to a Job

When I say this to an audience, I am always surprised at the subtle little gasp I hear from the room. When I say the same thing to employers, you should see their heads bounce up and down in agreement. I don't know why any healthy, capable person would ever think they are entitled to a job or a paycheck. If you can't earn it, you don't deserve it. It really is that simple.

The "Shock & Awe" of Termination

I was terminated. It's been many years now but I remember it as if it happened last week so I truly understand the shock and awe of job loss. I clearly understand the hurt, anger, grieving (although I did not recognize it as such at the time) of losing my job. I remember the frustration and desperation well.

I was once asked by a person I was counseling how long it had taken for me to overcome my termination. I had never been asked this question before and I had to lean back and take a moment to think about my response. Finally I said, "I don't think I have ever gotten over it."

I stand by that statement today which is why I think this job search thing is, to me, so important. I'm very good at, and proud of what I do. I genuinely believe it's because I lived the shock and awe that I am so passionate about helping you successfully manage this "job search thing."

Job Search is No Longer About Selection—It's About Preventing Elimination

In the "old days" of say, prior to the mid-1990s, job search was still about submitting a resume to a real, human person who would review your document and maybe give you a call or maybe not. Today the game has changed significantly.

As you now know, the chances of a real, human-person actually seeing the resume you submit are small, slim and possibly none. It very much depends on the size of the company and whether or not they have instituted the job search/people sorting software that is so prolific today.

Note on **Who Is Seeing Your Resume**

OR

Why I'm a Fan of Staffing Companies

When you send your resume to a professional staffing company (as opposed to a company looking to make a direct hire) a human person really does read and review your resume—no matter how BAD it might be. Understand that to a staffing company you are their inventory; you are what they have to sell so they can't afford to miss any diamonds (that's you) simply because you did not have the ability to put together a rock-their-world resume. In short: sending your resume to a staffing company means someone *will* look at it!

Job Search Business Cards

Speaking of "Seeking a New Opportunity" as noted in the Networking section above, the best way to inform the grocer, mechanic or accountant is to provide them with job search business cards.

Now be careful here. I see far too many "designer" business cards handed out for this very serious business of job search. The fact is job search is a highly conservative effort meaning a conservative resume and any other presentation materials you prepare must not "rock the boat" so to speak. What you consider appropriate or professional is not for YOU to decide. It's for the person on the other side of the desk to determine and — trust me here — you can't win. Go conservative and you can't lose.

Choose black or blue ink on a white business card. The front should have your name, the position or industry you are seeking, your email and your one best phone number. That's it. Simple. Clean. Professional.

On the back you may want to add a very few details taken from your resume that will gain the reader's attention but keep it short. The purpose of your job search business card is to make contact only. You sell yourself in person.

One last point: You should leave the house every day with 30 job search business cards on you and return at the end of the day with none. They do no good whatever if they remain in a box at home.

Sample Job Search Business Card

> ### Jerry Job Seeker
> Seeking a position in Staffing or
> Talent Acquisition
>
>
> JerryJobSeeker@email.com   212.123.4567

"Resumes are Unfair"

You already know this but I think it bears repeating: keep in mind that a resume, regardless of length or format, serves only one purpose — to initiate a dialog.

50% of All Resumes Contain Lies and Misrepresentations

Ask any HR person, business owner or staffing professional and they will confirm this statement. So don't lie. Do not misrepresent. Understand that Google is the new background check. And with commercial background investigations, reference checking and software search capabilities available today you will be found out.

And while I'm on the point, if you have something you aren't particularly proud of in your background, don't hesitate to bring it up to your interviewer at the end of the conversation after you have knocked their socks off with your ability to add value to the organization.

Many HR professionals have told me that they would have recommended a hire had they only told them at that first meeting that they had a bankruptcy or a DUI or a drug conviction (etc.) in their history. Recruiters have heard it all. This is not to say that your background won't impact whether you are hired or not. It will. But when a lie or misrepresentation is discovered by a source other than you at any point during the hiring process, everything thing else you have said is now suspect and you will receive no further consideration.

Compelling & Memorable (Make Me Money or Save Me Money!)

You already know this but it is also worth repeating: When you are able to express how you will Make Money or Save Money for your next employer, you will find that you have achieved Compelling and Memorable. This is what an employer WANTS to hear from you. When the job seeker's first questions are those related to salary, vacation, benefits and breaks - well, come on! Do I really have to say any more? You can show yourself out.

However, when you express that you understand how expensive it is to open the doors on a daily basis; when you can empathize with what an employer spends on wages, inventory, facilities, equipment, utilities, security, software, promotion, taxes and fees, transportation, travel and all the other costs associated with just being in business, you quickly go to the front of the line when being considered for your position.

Online Applications

In my counseling and speaking experience, many people come to me upset because unless they answer such-and-such question in an online application (usually an age-related question), they cannot move forward with the process (usually due to the need for a field to be populated prior to allowing the cursor to move to the next field).

I understand this concern and my only answer is that you, the job seeker, must determine whether you want to "pass" — not provide the information and therefore not apply for the position or "play," wherein you determine what the heck - might as well roll the dice and see what happens.

I will say this: by deciding not to play you already have a "no." Without trying, you don't know what the outcome might have been.

Where I can offer assistance is in the promise that if you use the tactics and techniques you learn in steps 1 and 2 (Accomplishments and Keywords) you will have a far better chance at success than if you didn't play.

Job Search is Tax Deductible

I'm certainly not an accountant but I can tell you that if you wander over to IRS.gov and search "job search expenses" there is a wealth of information available for you. You may even be able to deduct a portion of the cost of this book courtesy of Uncle Sam.

JOB SEARCH SCAMS

There are so many job search scams on the street and online that I recommend you simply Google the phrase. You will be astounded by what will come up.

The one scam that I do want to mention here is the 'job placement agency' that for a fee will *guarantee* you a job. Unless someone is able to sign a paycheck with your name on it they cannot guarantee you a job. Period. Don't be fooled. You've been warned.

Job!

Chapter 11

The Entry-Level/New College Graduate Resume

"Your work is going to fill a large part of your life, and the only way to be truly satisfied is to do what you believe is great work. And the only way to do great work is to love what you do. If you haven't found it yet, keep looking. Don't settle. As with all matters of the heart, you'll know when you find it."

Steve Jobs

If you are an entry-level job seeker and you skipped to this chapter please go back to the beginning of the book and read it in its entirety. The information that follows has little value unless you understand the mechanics of job search explained throughout the previous chapters. You will be glad you did!

Networking is King

Networking is still and always will be the first and best place to find a job, especially if you interned during your college career. The problem with networking for young people is that unless you have a family member or a personal friend in a position to introduce you into your chosen field, you probably have limited resources for making important contacts.

But Social Media is –Or Will Soon Be—King in Job Search

Networking aside, job search for entry-level positions has changed substantially in the past few years. With apps, social media and the ever-present online application, job search has gone totally mobile for a person seeking their first position.

But even as recruiters are maximizing the use of social media, it makes no difference how proficient you are on message boards or online forums if you don't have content to feed the beast. You know content is king so let's create some job search content that will blow the competition away.

Above, I insisted you read the rest of this book prior to moving into this chapter because it is important that you have a strong working knowledge of this 3 step job search process. You can use your new/recent graduate status only one time after which, everything that precedes this chapter will be needed for all future job searches and even job offers.

By learning the skills in this book and continuously maintaining an accomplishments journal you should never be at a loss while looking for work in the future. I don't want you to suffer what some your families have as a result of job loss.

Unless you just completed a nursing or pharmacy degree or your family owns the business, it is a tough job market for the new college grad these days. Many graduates are not finding work in their fields of choice and every semester, colleges across the country turn out another batch of competition for you to deal with. So the lessons here are crucial for you in finding and maintaining your next job.

Short-Form or Long-Form Resume?

If you are the über achiever who needs additional space to explain personal achievements, the 3 step process that is the message at the heart of this book will work well for you. Nevertheless, it is my experience that most new graduates are well served by an impressive, single page (or Short-Form) resume.

Review Jennifer Job Seeker's entry-level, architectural resume below to see how this format can work for you.

Job!

Jennifer Job Seeker

JenniferJobSeeker@email.com
Willing to Relocate/Travel 50%
Bilingual: English / Spanish

(123) 456-7890
Currently residing in Austin, TX
Non-Smoker

I am seeking an interview for a position as an Entry-level Architect with Gigantic Architects, Inc., reference # 12345.

OBJECTIVE STATEMENT

I am prepared to apply my scholastic experience to actual projects in a professional environment for the benefit of Gigantic Architects, Inc.; to be an asset to the company and be an active member of the architecture team. My near-term goal is to complete my licensing requirements working under an experienced senior architect.

SELECTED PERSONAL ACHIEVEMENTS

- Graduated from Texas A&M University with a Bachelor of Architecture degree.
- Soccer captain that lead my high school team to state championship and won the state title.
- Member of my high school 1-5A UIL Team Tennis state championship team.
- National Honor Society volunteer working with Habit for Humanity building houses.

RELEVANT EXPERIENCE

Planning Group, Phoenix, AZ   June-Sept 2014
Architecture Intern
- Participated and contributed on multi-million dollar Western Canal Path and design for the city of Tempe, AZ.
- Assisted Senior Architect with GIS mapping project for city of Phoenix, AZ.
- Reviewed plans for the City of Phoenix Planning Department

Study Abroad, Bonn, Germany   Fall Semester, 2012
Architecture Department, Texas A&M University
- Worked for the City of Bonn Planning Department to design pedestrian linkage between the city center and the Rhine River

Advanced Architecture Classes Taken
- Sustainable Design
- Urban Design
- Commercial Construction (II, III)

ACTIVITIES & HONORS

Phi Phi Phi National Sales & Marketing Fraternity
- Organized and produced marketing and fundraising projects resulting in over $23,000 donated to local charity.

Texas A&M Intramural Sports
Soccer Referee
- Refereed multiple soccer games for all skill levels on a weekly basis

Keywords: architecture architectural project manager architectural project management project architect staff architect architectural designer architectural design senior designer principal AutoCAD CAD Revit ADT IDP AIA licensed license calculation of load capacity emerging repair technologies structural reinforcements splices flitch plates epoxy anchors carbon-fiber mesh

The Entry-Level Accomplishment List

Having read this far, you already know the reason and value of taking a personal inventory to create an Accomplishments Statement. You might think you are too young to have any significant achievements but at your age an employer does not expect you to have discovered the cure for cancer—at least not yet. Let me explain with an all-too-common scenario.

In today's economy, many small business owners are struggling to get by. Success may be within reach but often every dollar generated is spent before it comes in. Even so, new staff is needed but bringing someone on board is a potentially costly investment and the owner cannot afford to make mistakes.

Picking through a pile of resumes, the owner comes across a graduate who worked part-time for a single company throughout his entire high school and college career and moved up the ranks to boot. That's impressive. It speaks to loyalty, reliability, responsibility, the ability to learn new processes and work with a team.

Now, assuming the resume shows the proper educational and/or skill set, this applicant definitely gets a phone call. Why? Because after determining the "hard skills" part of the requirements for the job (experience, education, internships, training or degree), the "soft skills" speak volumes about the kind of person the owner wants to hire.

Soft Skills?

So you may not have discovered the cure for cancer but you bring enormous value to an organization in the form of personal traits, also known as soft skills, which you learned growing up. These would include such highly prized qualities in an employee as common courtesy, attention to detail, loyalty, up to the challenge, good judgment, motivation, leadership, responsibility, being on time, initiative, thoughtfulness, curiosity, as well as the capacity to adapt to changing situations and thinking on your feet — to name just a few.

With that in mind, let's take a look at how former activities such as playing sports, participating in charitable events or even forming a musical group in high school or college looks to an employer who is seeking someone who "plays well with others," someone who thinks about more than just themselves; a person able to initiate a project.

Soft Skills & Accomplishments

You previously read in this book that accomplishments are compiled first from your own recollection followed by asking family, friends, co-workers, current or former supervisors, professors, clergy and anyone else you can think of who would be able to speak of your involvement in a group.

As a job seeker with little or no on-the-job experience to offer, it's imperative that you frame your accomplishments to clearly indicate your soft skills as well as the capabilities that will get you the job.

Look at Jennifer Job Seeker's resume above and note how many of accomplishment are listed without specifically pointing out any leadership or team player qualities. Nevertheless, it's easy for an employer to read between the lines and identify those traits. Use that as a template for your own resume.

· · ·

For the new or soon-to-be college graduate, it's worth repeating that you should make the effort to approach current or former professors to ask about any successes you had in the classroom. It is in the interest of professors to see that their students get hired and move on to bigger and better things. They are inherently motivated to assist you.

The question you need answered by anyone you approach to assess any achievements or accomplishments is this:

1. What impact did I have on the company, department, class or organization?
    Or, stated differently:

2. What difference did I make being in your class or working for you (or with you)?

The answer to these questions can be shaped into an accomplishment. (If the response from the person you ask really rocks, request a letter of recommendation.) Just remember the format for a completed accomplishment is a beginning, a middle and an end (or net result).

Mickey Ds & More About Soft Skills

Okay, you have obtained your degree, a professional rite of passage, and as you prepare your resume, you begin to think that revealing your stint at McDonald's or baby sitting in high school cheapens your profile.

Not at all!

Remember the young man in the small business owner story above, the one who worked one job throughout high school and beyond? That was a real person I worked with who, when he moved to New York in search of an internship in the recording industry, did not want to mention the company he had worked for all those years because it was not a "cool," music-industry related concern.

Recognizing the value of long-term service from a person so young, I insisted he retain that entry on his resume. That single item, along with his newly acquired studio skills and persistence, helped him land an internship and thus a career in the highly competitive world of professional recording and entertainment. (I'm pretty certain it will never appear on his resume again but it served the purpose at the time.)

So do not think that flipping burgers, working retail, in a warehouse or at any number of "uncool" places are not worthy of mention now that you have obtained your diploma. Did you know that Michael Dell, founder and chairman of Dell Computers, washed dishes in one of his first jobs? Or that Bill Gates was a page at the Washington state capitol? What about Johnny Depp having sold ballpoint pens over the phone or Kanye having been a sales assistant at Gap?

Get the picture?

Every person you hold in high regard, including your parents, began their journey somewhere. The question I want you to be able to answer after reviewing your completed resume is this: "Would I hire me?" If not, get back to work and don't quit until you have a resume that answers this question affirmatively.

Final Thoughts on Your Accomplishments Statement & Resume

Don't forget you are not done with your Accomplishments Statement and Resume until they are professionally formatted and ready for presentation.

As you draft your resume, don't hesitate to use the sample I have provided as your template.

In most cases the first accomplishment listed for any new college grad will be your recent graduation from college—and yes, you may then repeat it in the education section at the bottom of the page. No harm no foul. You deserve to be proud.

One last note—and I know you have heard this several times before. Clean up your social media profile if necessary so that it matches the person you describe on your resume.

I wish you great success.

Appendix

i.   Simple Job Search Launch/Checklist

ii. Sample Short-Form (One-Page) Resume (Jerry Job Seeker)

iii. Sample Entry-Level (New or Recent College Graduate) Resume (Jennifer Job Seeker)

iv. Sample Long-Form Resume (Jenny Job Seeker/3 pages)

v. Sample Completed Accomplishments Statement

Appendix i

The RickGillis.com (Very Simple) Job Search Check List

- Take a personal inventory of what you have to offer your next employer. Create an Accomplishments Statement of personal "bests" in your life. Take from your on-the-job experiences as well as academic, athletic, volunteer, charity, church & worship activities. When complete, prepare this document for formal presentation to your interviewer(s). Keep several copies with you at all times and one 'by the phone' to respond to phone inquiries.
- Invest a little bit of time and money and have some job search business cards printed. Include your name, the position you are seeking, your email address and phone number. That's it. Black or blue ink on white stock. Skip the cute designs.
- Create a Target List of companies you wish to pursue. Aim high! In the event the company of first choice is not hiring then pursue their nearest competitor. Your target list should include a minimum of 20 companies with 5 or more in your top tier.
- Create a Short-Form Resume* for the purpose of getting the appointment.
- Prepare a Long-Form Resume* to have available when receiving that first call from a recruiter asking "for more information."
- Upon receiving the call to interview prepare by viewing the company's annual report or SEC 10K report. Seek out any press releases for the past year on the corporate website. Search the company's name online. See what the public is saying about them. Seek them out in social media—especially LinkedIn.
- Thank you notes. Visit your local office supply and pick up a pack of Thank You cards. Handwrite and deliver them on the spot upon completion of your interview. Make yourself memorable. No one else is doing this!

* Keep copies of your Accomplishments Statement, Short-Form and Long-Form resumes on your phone or on any other mobile devices you carry.

Remember that preparation will make for a successful
in-person interview. Nothing will take the place of research.

Appendix ii • Sample Short-Form Resume

Jerry Job Seeker

JerryJobSeeker@email.com
Willing to relocate/travel 70%
Bilingual (English/Spanish)

123.456.7890
Currently residing in Houston, TX
Non-smoker

**I am seeking the position of International Sales Manager for
Giant Industrial Corporation reference #12345**

Objective Statement

As International Sales Manager for Giant Industrial Corporation I will significantly increase net revenues by implementation of current management and motivational techniques acquired through previous experience and continuing managerial education.

Selected Accomplishments

- Inherited and then overcame a $5,000,000 deficit in a badly designed national sales promotion by completely redesigning and developing a far superior plan resulting in a new system that reduced typical man hours the sales staff devoted to plan by 23% while increasing sales in excess of $1,000,000 per quarter.
- Saved over $500,000 annually in key sales communication systems and national transportation expenses while improving level of service to clientele.
- Dramatically reduced sales staff turnover by 28% due to more focused recruiting and selection process. Enhanced training and the creation of targeted management groups resulting in countless man-hour savings.
- Analyzed and merged more than 14 compensation plans into one corporate plan that resulted in a savings exceeding $270,000 the following fiscal year while continuing to fairly compensate the sales staff for their efforts.

Employment History

Giant National Employment Website, Atlanta, GA   Jan 2002 – Jan 2014
    Director, West Coast Sales
Giant National Employment Website is recognized as one of the leading employment websites worldwide.

Gulf Coast Group Internet, Houston, TX   1998 – 2001
    Sales Manager, South Central US
The Texas based Gulf Coast Group is one of the nation's leading providers of employment internet related solutions such as resume screening services and applicant tracking systems.

The Express Internet Company, New Orleans, LA   1997–1998
    Employment Internet Startup Consultant
The Express Internet Company, currently operating profitably in 27 markets in 13 states, offers turnkey Internet services from web design to network applications with staff of 33 employees.

Bachelor of Science Management, Park University, Parkville, MO
Veteran USAF, Honorable Discharge
Member, Board of Directors, Ronald McDonald House

Keywords: Sales marketing advertising networking consumer retention consumer survey website development website sales internet sales return on investment promotional campaign Houston, TX administrative assistant 3 years' experience articulate attention to detail multi-task professional appearance strong business etiquette college degree word excel power point quicken macromedia contribute bilingual

Appendix iii · Sample Entry-Level Short-Form Resume

Jennifer Job Seeker

JenniferJobSeeker@email.com
Willing to Relocate/Travel 50%
Bilingual: English/Spanish

(123) 456-7890
Currently residing in Austin, TX
Non-Smoker

**I am seeking an interview for a position as an Entry-level Architect with
Gigantic Architects, Inc., reference # 12345.**

OBJECTIVE STATEMENT
I am eager to apply my scholastic experience to actual projects in a creative environment for the benefit of Gigantic Architects, Inc. I am ready to be an asset to the company and be an active member of the architecture team. My near-term goal is to complete my licensing requirements working under an experienced senior architect.

SELECTED PERSONAL ACHIEVEMENTS
- Graduated from Texas A&M University with a Bachelor of Architecture degree.
- Soccer captain that lead my high school team to state championship and won the state title.
- Member of my high school 1-5A UIL Team Tennis state championship team.
- National Honor Society volunteer working with Habit for Humanity building houses.

RELEVANT EXPERIENCE
Planning Group, Phoenix, AZ   June-Sept 2014
Architecture Intern
- Participated and contributed on multi-million dollar Western Canal Path and design for the city of Tempe, AZ.
- Assisted Senior Architect with GIS mapping project for city of Phoenix, AZ.
- Reviewed plans for the City of Phoenix Planning Department
Study Abroad, Bonn, Germany   Fall Semester, 2012
Architecture Department, Texas A&M University
- Worked for the City of Bonn Planning Department to design pedestrian linkage between the city center and the Rhine River
Advanced Architecture Classes Taken
- Sustainable Design
- Urban Design
- Commercial Construction (II, III)

ACTIVITIES & HONORS
Phi Phi Phi National Sales & Marketing Fraternity
- Organized and produced marketing and fundraising projects resulting in over $23,000 donated to local charity.
Texas A&M Intramural Sports
Soccer Referee

- Refereed multiple soccer games for all skill levels on a weekly basis

Keywords: architecture architectural project manager architectural project management project architect staff architect architectural designer architectural design senior designer principal AutoCAD CAD Revit ADT IDP AIA licensed license calculation of load capacity emerging repair technologies structural reinforcements splices flitch plates epoxy anchors carbon-fiber mesh

Appendix iv · Sample Long-Form Resume (3 Pages)

Jenny Job Seeker

123-456-7890
Willing to travel 50%
Bilingual (Spanish)

jennyjobseeker@email
Currently residing Cleveland, OH
Non-Smoker

I am seeking a position with HPS.

OBJECTIVE STATEMENT
As a result of my skills, experience and education I am capable of being a long-term member of your team by providing empathic support for pet owners, enhancing relationships with clients, and improving efficiency in documentation and communication.

SELECTED PERSONAL ACHIEVEMENTS
- As a service writer at Atwater's, I carefully considered the owner's needs, desires, safety, budget, and equipment condition leading to the highest average repair invoices and being the most requested employee in the service department
- Completed over 150 hours in a clinical counseling internship at Island Seminary resulting in consistently positive reviews from my clinical supervisor based upon collaboration with other trainees, client case notes, treatment plans, clinical skills and the ability to develop client rapport
- Established strong customer relationships at TMO resulting in repeat sales and service requests leading to an increase in profits every year, both in product and service, resulting in a significant store expansion in 2007
- Trained employees of 6 different bicycle shops in effective selling of service which resulted in: raising the average invoice amount, improving communication skills, increasing attention to detail, and gaining empathy for the customer's situation

EMPLOYMENT HISTORY
SGW School, Liberty, Ohio   August 2012-Present
After Care Coordinator, Extended Care Assistant Teacher, & Substitute Teacher
SGW is a non-profit, non-discriminatory educational organization, welcoming children from preschool through grade eight of all races, religions and national origins.
- Provide structure and care for up to 60 students for up 3 hours after the school day
- Ohio Department of Education Student Aide certified and first aid certified
- Assisted in leading a class of 8 preschool and kindergarteners in a sit down meal and structured afternoon of activities

Atwater's Bike Shop, Akron, Ohio   2003-2004 & 2008-2012
Service Manager
Ohio's oldest and best known bicycle shop has four locations throughout Ohio, and has served their customers with the best in bicycle sales and service since 1940.
- Managed the work of 10 service staff at one of the largest volume bicycle shops in the country, leading to the assembly, service and tuning of over 10,000 bikes per year
- Developed and organized a used bicycle and parts system that went from selling $1,000 of used bicycles to revenue of over $15,000 in bicycles and $3,000 in parts per year
- Converted and retrained a paper-based service department to a fully computer-based system resulting in less paper work along with more accurate estimates, work process scheduling, invoices, inventory, and customer history

- Created employee training and quality control documents leading to over 100 pages of original material
- Proved to be a well-rounded and helpful worker leading to roles as: manager, salesperson, cashier, mechanic, service writer, bicycle fitter, warehouse staff, inventory processor, warranty specialist, new parts buyer, janitor, equipment deliverer, employee trainer and bicycle shop customer service consultant

River Consulting, Cuyahoga Falls, Ohio   2009
Freelance HME Manual Editor
River Consulting offers full service consulting that provides accreditation preparation services for Home Medical Equipment (HME), home health organizations seeking accreditation, and compliance with applicable regulations.

- Edited home medical companies' compliancy, policy and procedure manuals, including creating original customized policies, ensuring ability for Medicare funding
- Assembled professional paper hardcopy and computer-based manuals for each contracted company

Technical Multisport Operations, Columbus, Ohio   2005-2008
Service Manager and Assistant Store Manager
TMO is a professional bicycle and triathlon retail store, providing a niche product line, excellent customer support, and attract demanding, educated customers.

- Contributed to the realized increase in profits every year, both in product and service, resulting in a significant store expansion in 2007
- Established strong customer relationships resulting in repeat sales and service requests leading to be contracted as the first-ever salaried manager in 20 years of operation
- Created a successful customer loyalty program to attract and retain customers resulting in its continued use for almost 10 years
- Provided consultation to small business ownership, which improved efficiency, profitability, and the level of customer service

Spring Ministry Life Center, Cleveland, Ohio   2006
Pastoral Counseling Intern and Volunteer
Spring Ministry staff and volunteers connect with at-risk teens to share God's truth and to equip them with the tools to experience real life change.

- Built trusting relationships with youth in need
- Led activities and games, mentored junior high and senior high students, led Bible studies, and transported students safely to and from their homes
- Created an organizational system for inventory and usage of the center's computer lab

Coastal Counseling, Columbus, Ohio   2005
Counselor Trainee
Through our more than 40 counselors, coaches, and masters student interns we are able to make professionally trained, biblically sound counseling and coaching affordable.

- Diagnosed personal and mental difficulties, created treatment plans, and counseled children and adults, while under supervision
- Collaborated with other trainees in their diagnoses and treatment plans during supervisory meetings
- Treated difficulties such as: anger management, anxiety, attention deficit disorder, depression, family trauma, and substance abuse

Minsk International School, Minsk, Belarus   2001-2002
      Science and Mathematics Educator
MIS is a private non-profit institution that offers high quality education in the English language for students from three years through eighteen years of age.
- Planned and taught 7 classes a day in science and mathematics to children ages 5-16 at a school for international students
- Held parent-teacher conferences to inform parents of their children's academic progress and advise them on any need for further assistance
- Served as the lead administrator for two weeks during the school director's absence, and successfully navigated a conflict between a parent and the school

Major University, Canton, Ohio   1999-2000
      Co-Student Activities Council Director
Major's S.A.C. creates and promotes campus environments that result in multiple opportunities for student learning and development
- Budgeted, planned, promoted and supervised the social activities of a college campus of 2,000 students
- Increased the number of student volunteers in my committee three-fold in a one-year period
- Delegated to as many as fifty people at a time leading to the successful hosting of two 500 seat dinner events
- Became the top educational technology student resulting in being chosen by the Major College Education Department staff to be a teacher's assistant for a computer and technology training course, with special focus in Microsoft Office and website creation

Education History
Master of Arts in Counseling, Island Theological Seminary, Youngstown, Ohio
Bachelor of Arts in Liberal Arts, Major University, Canton, Ohio

Appendix v

Janet Job Seeker Personal Accomplishments

JanetJobSeeker@email.com
212.456.7890

- Completed special assignments on inventory phase-outs, unallocated materials, and obsolete inventory resulting in savings to the company of $1,500,000.
- Improved operation scores for district to 90% from 82% in prior years as a result of group and individual coaching of district front line employees.
- Provided a 12% profit increase from previous management by marketing and establishing new institutional accounts.
- Successfully trained tri-state team of over 800 managers, sales reps, technicians, and support staff on key company programs which resulted in improved service levels by 10%, improved operations processes and increased customer satisfaction.
- Led team to be first dedicated repair center in the country to be ranked in the top 5 in customer satisfaction by developing an action plan that included team participation.
- Improved past due performance of vendors by implementing a daily expedite program. Result: Logistics performance improved from 43% past due orders to 6% within 5 months.
- Led nation in an 18% improvement of sales in electronics by training store personnel on educating the customer on product functionality and reliability.
- Performed annual performance reviews and facilitated employee's creation of individual development plans which led to increased employee satisfaction and motivation by 15% over previous management team.

About the Author

Rick Gillis, as a pioneer of 21st century job search, was instrumental in launching the first job board serving the greater Houston, TX area. Rick has been noted & quoted, heard & seen in The Wall Street Journal, Forbes.com, The Houston Chronicle, San Francisco Chronicle, BlackEnterprise.com, DallasNews.com, CIO.com, CFO.com, ComputerWorld, USATodayCollege, HerCampus.com, HuffingtonPost; has been heard on NPR, PBS and countless online/radio & TV stations across the country; has hosted employment television and Rick Gillis Employment Radio in the Houston/Dallas markets. Rick writes support and opinion pieces for CIO.com and Salary.com.

Rick has been involved in or has intimate knowledge of the technological and "mechanical" aspects of the employment business to include resume development—specifically, his resume submission strategy: the short-form format followed by the long-form resume; employment advertising; recruiting; pre-employment assessments; networking and social networking sites; age-discrimination issues; the human resources function; best practices as they apply to management; diversity considerations; legal issues; staffing companies; web based applicant-tracking systems, resume filtering systems and, of course, Internet employment protocols.

Passionate about his topic, Rick appears across the country. High energy, actionable, focused, motivating and on-point are the terms best used to describe Rick's live presentations.

For more information visit: www.RickGillis.com

Rick's Keywords!

Keywords: rickgillis.com, job search, resume, Pre-Resume™, employment, career, employment trends, unemployment, BLS, Bureau of Labor Statistics, entry-level job search, mature job seeker, age discrimination in job search, interviewing, networking, online application, skilled trade, keywords, personnel, staffing company, salary negotiation, cover letter, thank you card, assessment, HR, Human Resources, moms reentering the workforce, race and employment, job application, profession, C-Suite, accomplishments, baby boomer, career change, job fair, job boards, LinkedIn, career planning, compensation, Gen Y, Millennial, internship, hidden job market, job scams, passive job search, active job search, references, career coach, succession planning, temporary employment, employment professional, employment correspondent, workforce contributor, social media and job search, social media in job search, apps and job search